# cherokee valley so wild

# OTHER BOOKS BY JOSEPH E. DABNEY

*Mountain Spirits*

*More Mountain Spirits*

*HERK: Hero of the Skies*

*Smokehouse Ham, Spoon Bread & Scuppernong Wine*

*Food, Folkore & Art of Lowcountry Cooking*

# cherokee valley so wild

Joseph E. Dabney

Bilbo
Books
Publishing
Athens, Georgia

Cherokee Valley So Wild

Bilbo Books Publishing
www.BilboBooks.com

ISBN- 978-0-9800108-7-9
ISBN- 0-9800108-7-X

Printed in the United States of America

# cherokee valley so wild

This Book is dedicated to
Professor J. B. Tate
Long time Historian of the Cherokee People
Including the Sad Trail of Tears

## PROLOGUE

Pa's funeral near bout turned into a disaster. The skies turned dark and gloomy just as we were about to start the service. The sun disappeared behind huge clouds of passenger pigeons; wave after wave they came, millions of them, thundering across the sky in a seemingly endless stream for more than an hour at a speed of a mile a minute, someone said.

All of us were relieved when the last of the birds kept flying south, without stopping. Even so, they created an uneasiness among our four wagon loads of missionary families including four kids.

Everything had happened so quickly that it left a blur in my fourteen-year-old mind and I had trouble taking it all in. My name, by the way, is Little Jon Merion; I was named for my preacher pa. Most folks call me Jon Boy.

The tragedy began when Pa, driving the lead wagon, fell violently ill, forcing us to pitch camp right off the road. The chills and fevers clobbered him hard, bilious fever I heard it called.

Ma and I stayed by his side throughout his painful torment, caressing him with cool towels, making onion poltices for his chest, and reading to him from the Bible, including one of his favorite passages from Saint John:

> *"Let not your heart be troubled; ye believe*
> *in God, believe also in me. In my house are*
> *many mansions; if it were not so, I would have*
> *told you so. I go now to prepare a place for you . . ."*

The only ray of sunshine that sad day here in the southwest Virginia wilds came about sundown when two riders came galloping up on black horses from the south, trailed by their two dogs. The man dismounted and approached Ma, who was sitting in a chair near our wagon. He had a light brown skin and straight black hair that came down almost to his shoulders. He was trailed by two dogs.

"Beg your pardon, ma'am," he said. "I noticed your wagons. You all wouldn't be the missionaries coming from Charlottesville, would you?"

"We are indeed, sir," Ma said, standing up and struggling to get hold of herself after hours of crying.

"I'm Chief Talking Rock from the Hi-wass'ee Valley in the Cherokee country, ma'am, and this is my wife, Gilda Golden-feather. We've come to help guide you folks down to the land of the Cherokees." He reached out his hand in a show of friendship. Someone told me later they thought the chief was a mixed-breed Indian.

"Thanks be to God," Ma said in a trembly voice, daubing

her bloodshot eyes with her hanky. "We're so proud to see you. We've just buried my preacher husband and we're still in a state of shock."

"Awfully sorry to hear about your terrible misfortune, ma'am," he said, bowing his head. "Our deepest condolences."

He seemed sincere and I was amazed at his youthful looks and his clear use of the English language.

Mother started sobbing again and the chief's wife came up and wrapped her arms around Ma in a most affectionate way, holding her tight for a long while.

The next morning, I was astonished to find that Ma had suddenly snapped out of her terrible gloom. "Their coming was an answer to our prayers, son," Ma said, "a sign that the Lord was looking down on us."

I agreed that it was a mighty powerful sign and sure enough a result of her near constant prayers. I'd said "amen" a time or two, but I'm not yet at the age of praying out loud. What praying I do, I do in my heart. An unspoken prayer, I've heard it called. Ma had told me that a silent prayer was perfectly acceptable in the eyes of the Lord.

When the chief asked Ma if she might wish to turn around and go back to our old home in Charlottesville, she shocked us all when she stood up ramrod straight and declared in a strong voice, "No, Chief Talking Rock; I favor proceeding directly on to the Cherokee country, the sooner the better."

I could have kissed Ma right then and there, except we don't do much kissing in our family. "It's the Lord's will that we go on," she told our crowd. "The good Cherokees likely still need us, even if Reverend Merion will not be with us."

The young chief appeared amazed like the rest of us by Ma's renewed vision. "God bless you, Mistress Merion," he said. Excitement spread through our crowd and the young chief spoke up. "Folks, let's plan to get on the road tomorrow. Let's get the wagons packed tonight, so we can head out right after breakfast in the morning."

We awoke to a loud blast from the fox horn blown by Goliath Dan Haughton, our German wheelwright. And right after we had breakfast the chief gave us our marching orders.

"I'll be taking over the first wagon with Mistress Merion and Jon-Boy," he said. "The other three wagons will continue in the hands of the same drivers." He added that he wanted his wife, Gilda Golden-feather, to join Hawk-eye Hawkins, our carpenter, as advance scouts on the black horses, seeking places to stop for the night plus grassy grazing land for our eighteen horses and the cow. "And any foodstuffs you can find along the way would be wonderful," he said.

Although it was left unsaid, Comfort Carreker, wife of

Conrad Carreker, our blacksmith, would continue milking their Jersey cow that was tied to the back of wagon number 4.

Ma prayed a brief prayer and we climbed aboard out wagons. It was the year 1821 and we all knew that we were sure on our way to a new world . . .

# CHAPTER ONE

## Meeting New Friends at the Great Tell-i'co
### *(A month later on the trail)*

I was enjoying being boss of Wagon 3 after Mister Roarty suffered a serious wrist injury back up the trail apiece
and Chief Talking Rock picked me to take his place. Ma
thought I was too young to do the job, but Talking Rock
told her I was growing up fast and that I could handle the
job.

We had reached the tail end of the Great Smoky Mountains the night before. I woke up early, pulled on my bro-
gans, jumped down from our Conastoga wagon and went
down to the camp fire, leaving Ma to sleep some more.

I got up just in time to see our big wheelwright, Goliath
Dan Haughton, tootin' his fox horn get-up call. It seemed
a little late; most everyone had already roused themselves

since we were nearing the Great Tell-i'co, the ancient entryway connecting the Cherokee Over Hill Towns in East
Tenn-a'see that we had been passing in recent weeks, to
the Indians' Middle Towns up ahead.

Further on, to the south, I learned, were the sad ruins of
the Cherokee Lower Towns. Their villages at the headwaters of the Savannah River were first burned to the ground
and their fields of corn were chopped down by the bayonets of the brutish British troops from Charleston.

"That was in the seventeen-hundreds," Talking Rock
declared. "It was a horrible foretaste of similar destruction
the Britishers and white American Una'kas would later
rain down on the Cherokee Upper Towns including the
ancient capital of Chota and hundreds of Indian villages
situated on the banks of rivers flowing into the Tenn-a'see,
the Cherokees' grand river."

But on this morning all our people were in a fine frame
of mind as we prepared to resume our trek to the Hi-
wass'ee Valley. I was getting hungry and I was glad that
Gilda Golden-feather was stacking up griddle cakes for us
and singing "Amazing Grace" at the same time.

Everyone turned their heads when we heard pounding
hoof beats. Riding fast and furious toward us was a young
blond-headed fellow atop a strawberry roan. He came to
a quick stop, dismounted and introduced himself as Reverend Merlin Montgomery. Talking Rock brought him

straight to Ma and they said their howdys.

"Where do you hail from, Reverend Montgomery?" Ma asked.

"I'm a native of Scotland, ma'am, but I came here from Charleston, down in the Carolina Low Country, where I've been studying at a seminary. I'm being sent as a missionary to the Cherokees in the Hi-wass'ee Valley."

"Fancy that! " Ma said, a bit startled. "So are we. We came down from Virginia. Unfortunately, we lost my husband several weeks ago on the trail in Virginia. He died of severe fevers and chills."

"Terribly sorry to hear of your awful misfortune, Mistress Merion. Terribly sorry," he said.

Ma introduced me to our visitor and he gave me a strong handshake. But he sure didn't look like a preacher man, being so young and wearing plain duds, not the dark suit that you'd expect of a Man of God.

"Reverend Montgomery," Ma said. "Why don't you ride the rest of the way with us in our wagon? Son Jon here is our driver."

"That's awfully kind of you, Ma'am," he said. "Wonderful idea! I'd like to do that. And by the way, y'all can just call me Merlin."

I decided right off that Merlin would be mighty good company and could help me run our wagon so long as he understood who was in charge.

At noontime, Chief Talking Rock turned his lead wagon into a grove of chestnut trees overlooking a swift moving stream. It was a cool valley and we were happy to take a noontime break after four hours on the hot dusty roadway.

"Don't that water look invitin'!" Kindness Haughton declared. "What might be its name?"

"This is the Tell-i'co River," Talking Rock said. "And that's the Tell-i'co Plains straight ahead. The Great Tell-i'co was one of the Cherokees' great mother towns early on in the Cherokee Nation."

"That was back when the Indian nation flourished in all its national glory, wasn't it?" asked Conrad Carreker, our studious German blacksmith.

"You are absolutely right, Conrad," Talking Rock said. "You obviously have read up on Cherokee history. Yes, that was indeed the period before the Europeans came in and messed things up for our people with smallpox, firewater and land greed."

After the noontime break, the chief gathered us in front of his lead wagon. "Just ahead, folks, is the Un-i'coi Turnpike. That'll take us through that big mountain gap ahead."

Back on the road, we came up to the turnpike entryway. It was a big disappointment. A wizened old white man was standing guard, backed up by another guard dressed in overalls, both toting long Kentucky hog rifles. I thought it right strange, with us going into the Cherokee Nation, and here were white men standing guard on the entryway. In a little shack sat another white fellow, an older gentleman in a coat and tie. I reckoned he was the boss man.

"Hello, Abe," Talking Rock said as he shook hands with the man in the shack.

"Welcome back, Chief," the old man replied. Later on, Talking Rock told us that Abe Jackson was one of five white Georgians who were operating the pike under a contract from the Cherokee National Council. "It follows the Indians' old Overhill Trading Path," he said. "The owners widened the trail with a gang of slaves," he said. "That helped speed up travel for drovers running pigs, cattle, turkeys and geese by the thousands through here every year, mostly from Tenn-a'see and Kentuck, headed to Augusta and Charleston."

"Abe," Talking Rock said, "I'm bringing in these four wagon loads of missionaries from Virginia."

"That'll be a dollar each for your four wagon teams," the old man said, "plus twenty five cents apiece for the extra horses and ten cents for the cow." Talking Rock pulled out his deerskin pouch and fished out some silver coins.

As we were pitching camp for the night, I noticed a bunch of dark skinned folks coming our way on the pike from the east. They were walking in a straight line headed by what looked like a papa and his wife, followed by an older man bent with age, perhaps the grandpa, and two young boys. The father was carrying a sack over his shoulder. I could see they had much darker skin than Chief Talking Rock, who of course is a mixed-breed. Then it came clear to me: "*They're full-blood Cherokees!*" I said to myself. I knew it right off. The first I'd ever seen. Nobody told me. I just figured it out on my own from what I had read before we began our trip.

"Good evening!" Goliath Dan said as he held up his open hand in friendship to the travelers. The Indians halted in their tracks and grinned back. It was plumb clear that they didn't speak our language and, of course, none of us other than Talking Rock and Gilda, who were in their wagon, could speak theirs. The men wore red bandanas wrapped around their heads. Turbans I heard they were called. And the dark-skinned elderly man had two big coins hanging from his ears, twice the size of silver doubloons!

"Con'a-sau'ga," the Cherokee papa said, pointing toward the west.

"He's telling you that's where they're going, Dan," Kindness Haughton said. "They're headed to Con'a-sau'ga. Ain't that over in Tenn-a'see?"

Goliath Dan pulled out his large hunting knife from his belt and drew a line in the red sand showing the turnpike heading east. He marked an "X" and said, *"Hi–wass'ee."* Then, pointing to himself and the others, said again, "Go Hi-wass'ee." The Cherokee papa grinned and nodded. The adults wore leather moccasins, but the two boys had on leather moccasins and wore tiny kilts that covered their privates. The woman had on a bright blue frock and the men wore deerskin pants and hunting shirts.

The old man with the big earrings drew the most stares. His face was covered with wrinkles, surely a man of many winters, as the Cherokees would tell it. But I kept thinking about his slitted ears. He must have suffered terrible pain as a young lad when his earlobes got sliced open. But I'd heard that Cherokees from childhood on were taught to never flinch despite pain.

"Miz Rebecca, Missionary Merlin!" Goliath Dan yelled, "come over here and meet these Cherokees!"

About that time, Talking Rock came out of his wagon, tipped his big hat right mannerly like and spoke some words to them in Cherokee. Then he called Merlin over and introduced him to the family. Merlin pulled out his black Bible and held it up high. They clearly understood and the man shook Merlin's arm.

I thought it was awful strange of the Cherokee, taking hold of Merlin's arm just below the elbow. Merlin appeared right puzzled at first, too, but then he returned the shake in the same manner, holding the Cherokee's forearm. "That's the Cherokee way of greeting one another," Talking Rock said.

I could see that Merlin was right touched, too, since this was probably his first time to meet up with full-blood Cherokees, and right on the outer fringe of the Indian nation. Merlin told us later he felt a tingling sensation going through his body like a little bolt of lightning as he shook arms and gazed into the eyes of the Indian man.

Merlin then reached over and shook arms with the old man with the huge earrings. Talking Rock motioned for the rest of our crowd to go over to shake arms with the others. I decided to join in the arm shaking, so I grabbed the arm of the Cherokee boy my size and we pumped our arms up and down and danced around at the same time.

The whole crowd, our bunch and their bunch, now in a circle, broke into big laughs and we all clapped our hands as we danced around in a circle.

It went on that way for a little while and then Preacher Merlin called for a word of prayer before we parted. He asked everyone to join hands.

*"Creator God, you have brought us to this place . . . We are nearing our life's destiny. Look over our little band, Lord Jehovah, and keep watch over us and the Cherokees we are seeking to minister to, including this little family."*

Talking Rock moved near Merlin and commenced linkstering his words to the Indians. I could see it came as a shock to the young missionary from Charleston who lost his timing for a few moments as he heard his words being repeated in Cherokee. Then he got started again:

*"Lord, give us the strength and compassion and wisdom to bring your word to these wonderful people. Help us to love them and teach them. And Lord, if it be your will, please help us and our poor horses cross that mighty mountain gap tomorrow . . Amen."*

All our crowd shouted a loud *A-MEN!*

The back end of Merlin's prayer took me by surprise but it needed saying, I reckon, since Talking Rock told us the gap would be a right mean climb .

Merlin knew the Cherokee words for goodbye—*do'nada-go'hvi*—"Until we see each other again," and he uttered them along with a departing wave. The Indians responded with the same expression, along with sweet smiles.

As the full-blood family began leaving one by one with

the father in the lead, I guess I shed a tear or two myself. I waved a few little waves to my new friend and looked a long time as the family moved into the distance and almost out of sight. I could see my young Cherokee friend looking back, too, up until the family disappeared behind a clump of trees at a bend in the road. A lump rose up in my throat that caused a tight swelling in my windpipe.

"Well now, Mister Merlin," said Goliath Dan, breaking the spell, "looks like you've done made yourself some friends amongst the Cherokees."

"It would appear," Merlin replied. "Wonder what they really thought?"

"Oh, they liked you," Talking Rock said. "Couldn't you tell? They loved your sincerity, and I predict they'll likely come to your services, should you continue to approach them in a humble and respectful spirit."

"But I must confess to you, Merlin," the chief added, "I skipped over that word 'pagan' when I was linkstering your talk. I don't know what that word translates to in Cherokee."

We didn't linger long after supper but said our prayers and went straight to bed. Talking Rock had urged us to do just that since crossing the Un-i'coi Gap, I heard, would be a very hard day indeed.

# CHAPTER TWO

## A Wild Crossing of the Un-i'coi Gap

I felt sorry for our horses. Climbing up the turnpike's Un-i'coi Gap, all of my team were huffing and puffing, their noses flaring, their mouths foaming, and their flat backs steaming with sweat.

But you had to give them credit. They didn't display a lazy bone in their bodies that I could tell. They seemed near out of breath at times under the scorching heat, yet they kept on pulling without a flinch.

The trail narrowed to the point where it looked to be only wide enough for a wagon to clear the trees on either side. Then ever so often, we'd pass deep drop-offs. When we reached a little flat spot big enough for our four wagons, Talking Rock called a halt.

"Folks," he said, "we're coming onto a rougher climb ahead and we need to lighten the load. I want you women and children to get out and walk from here to the top." Hawkeye Hawkins, our Scot carpenter, riding one of the black horses, joined the Roartys in leading the group up the turnpike trail.

I was mighty grateful that he allowed Merlin to stay in my wagon to help me stay on the straight and narrow. And with his shirt off, I saw he had plenty of muscles to work the brake handle on my right—just in case the wagon should start rolling backwards.

As we resumed our gap climb, drop-offs to the right side loomed deeper and darker. "Scary over here, Jon-Boy," Merlin allowed. "Looks like a chasm from hell."

I was too busy to ask him what "chasm" meant; I'd already become acquainted with what hell meant. Merlin yelled again: *Be careful, Jon, and keep the horses over toward your side, if you don't mind!*

I realized that all we needed for a disaster to occur would be for one of the horses to lose his footing and cause our wagon to tilt over and go tumbling down a sheer cliff. I didn't want to think about it, but I tightened up the reins in my sweaty hands and kept our wagon to the left as far as I could.

After what seemed forever—but was just over an hour— we reached a straight stretch of road spread out wide and flat and with room enough to accommodate all four wagons. "Is this the top of the gap?" I asked Talking Rock as he got down from his lead wagon.

"Sure is, Jon-Boy."

"Hoo-ray! " I shouted.

Everyone tied up their horses and took a walk up to the lookout.

"Lord have mercy! " Comfort Carreker shouted as we reached the crest. "Feels like we're perched up in heaven, looking down on God's world below."

"This must be the view of the Twenty-Nine Mountains that the old traders wrote about," Talking Rock said, looking over the thin blue haze and ridges on top of ridges stretching far into the distance. Merlin agreed. "No wonder the Cherokees fell in love with this country when they first arrived here," he said. "They called it *Shaconage*, I understand, '*Mountains of the blue smoke*'."

Conrad Carreker spoke up: "And don't forget what the old botanist John Bartram found when he visited the Smokies in the late 1700's, that nowhere else on the North American continent was plant life so diverse as in the Smoky Mountains."

Ma stood there and gazed into the distance for a long time like all of us, glorying at the amazing mountain ridges. "They're swelling like ocean waves," she said. "And oh, so gorgeous! " Of a sudden she broke out in song and the whole crowd joined in on the chorus:

*God moves in a mysterious way*
*His wonders to perform;*
*He plants His footsteps in the sea,*
*And rides upon the storm.*

"Out yonder in the valleys spread out before us," Talking Rock said, "are the Middle Towns of the old Cherokee Nation. All that territory was well known to the Scotch-Irish and German Tenn-a'seeans and the Welsh and English mountaineers of Virginia who took their long rifles across to Kings Mountain and whipped the Tory forces during the Revolutionary War."

"Now wait just a minute," Goliath Dan piped up. "The way I heard it, the only real British Tory at Kings Mountain was the commander, a Scot major by the name of Patrick Ferguson."

"You're tee-totally right, Dan," Talking Rock replied, looking a little sheepish. "Ferguson's fighters were mostly Scotch-Irish lads the Brits had recruited in lower South Carolina to fight the Tory cause."

"In other words," Ma said, "the battle pitted the mountaineer Scotch-Irish against the Low Country Scotch-Irish?"

"For a true fact, Mistress Rebecca! " Talking Rock said. "Like I told y'all before, the patriot fighters who came back through here after the Kings Mountain battle took vengeance on the poor Cherokees in the Middle Towns and the Over Hill Towns that we passed up in East Tenn-a'see."

"Why was that?" somebody asked.

"Because the Cherokee National Council had decided that our warriors would fight with the British Crown in the Revolutionary War. The white sharpshooters resented that and took it out on the poor Cherokee women and children left behind in their little cabins around here."

Talking Rock broke up the classroom session. "For the next few miles," he said, "we'll be going downhill and you drivers need to get some strong backs to man your right-hand brake handles."

I was a little worried from the start about the downhill drive ahead, being as I had no experience in mountain gap driving. But Chief Talking Rock had told me I was certainly qualified, due to my size and intelligence. Even so, I was mighty happy that Merlin would be helping me out as my brake man. Before we departed, Merlin and I went around and inspected the big blocks of wood intended to scrub up against the iron tires to slow down the wagon if needed.

The trip down the gap's east side quickly turned treacherous. We skirted some sheer rock falloffs where we could have plunged to our death. I kept a sweaty hold on the rawhide reins and we slowed up a bit. After a while, though, Talking Rock and Goliath Dan's wagons went clear out of sight. I told Ma that when we topped the next rise, I was aiming to catch up. "Now take it easy, son," she said with her usual caution, then returned to the inside of the wagon. I yelled for Merlin to keep a steady hand on the brakes.

Well, by golly, when I lightly popped the leather to my horses' backsides, they commenced trotting. Halfway down the little decline we started rolling right smartly, making up for the lost time in a mighty fine way. Another small rise led to a steep decline. Suddenly, trees started spinning by in a blur.

"*Pull on the brakes, Merlin!*" I yelled.

"*I'm pulling Jon, I'm pulling! How bout slowing down those horses?*" A momentary thrill raced through my body as we dashed madly down the crooked trail. Then fear took over. Lord Have Mercy! We were whirling past deep drop-offs. Ma stumbled up to our bench as the wagon swayed from side to side. She looked frantic and yelled again for me to slow down. Then she grabbed a cross bar for dear life.

I was shocked when I saw that the wagon was pushing the horses down the hill! "*Lord save us!*" I yelled, praying my first ever spoken prayer. "*Else we're gon'a die a terrible death out here on this lonely mountain and we'll never get to help the Cherokees!*"

The Lord didn't answer. I guess He couldn't hear me on account of all the noise coming from the screaming brakes and the snorting horses that were bellowing something dreadful. Blood was streaming from the backsides of the two nearest us where the single trees were scrubbing against their legs. Terror filled their eyes and they twisted their heads this way and that, being hurled against the wagon tongue, stumbling and catching their footing and stumbling again. The wagon was totally out of control.

"*Lock the brakes tight, Merlin!*" I screamed.

"*They're broke, Jonnie. The brake shoes are worn through!*"

"*Oh my Lord in heaven!*" I ground my teeth and reckoned my time on earth was about to come to a pitiful end. "*Please, Lord, take my soul and that of Ma,*" I prayed, "*and let us join up with Pa in heaven."*

About that time, as we rounded a curve, I looked up and saw the first two wagons looming up straight ahead; Talking Rock's wagon number 1 had turned left into a flat open bottomland. But the second one—Goliath Dan's—had come to a dead halt straight in front of us. I crawled way out on the wagon tongue to the two front horses and jerked their bits to the left. Just in time, we swerved to the left and missed Dan's wagon but we skidded sideways into Talking Rock's rig. Jolting to a sudden stop, I felt myself whirling through the air, flying right over the horses' heads and landing in a bony pile near where Talking Rock and Gilda Golden-feather were sitting.

For a few moments I lay there in shock. My heart was racing to beat all and I noticed the right hand wheels kept spinning since the wagon ended up on its left side. I saw Gilda feeling her ribs to see if they were broken. Meanwhile, Merlin came crawling down from the back end of our wagon. He had held on, praise Jesus.

*"Where's Ma?"* I yelled.

*"She's right here in the wagon, safe and secure!"* Merlin yelled back. Then he brought her out. I didn't see a single scratch on her. Hallelujah!

"How are you, son?" she asked.

"I'm fine, Ma, now that I see you're not injured."

I took time to thank the Heavenly Father for answering my prayers in a surprising way! Then I helped Ma find a place to sit down in the grass next to Gilda and Talking Rock.

Conrad Carreker's wagon number 4 rolled up alongside us and he jumped out and dashed to Ma and me and then to Merlin and Talking Rock and Gilda, making sure we were all right.

Chief Talking Rock managed to get upon his right knee and then stood up, apparently not badly hurt. He looked over at me. Although I had some cuts and bruises about my face and arms, I put up a good front, forcing myself to display a big grin.

"My Lord, Jon-boy," the chief said, "you look like you've been sortin' wildcats!" He quickly added, in a serious tone, "I'm mighty proud to see you walking around in one piece, boy. And the same for your dear mother."

"Thank the Lord," Ma said, getting back up and brushing dust off her dress.

Merlin came out without a scratch and I took that as a sign that the Lord had big things in mind for the young missionary in the future.

I was full of embarrassment and was waiting to get romped on by Talking Rock for letting my horses get out of control. Instead, he patted me on the back, affectionate like, and said, "Jon, you did good, boy, considering the circumstances, and you and your ma and Merlin showed powerful bravery. I'm mighty proud of you all."

Well, praise the Lord. He must've realized that I'd already flogged myself in my mind dozens of times. Which was a true fact, as Talking Rock would put it. Right then and there, the Cherokee chief taught me a powerful lesson, that there's no call to put a body down for something he's awfully ashamed of and more'n likely has already slapped himself in his own mind many times, over and over and over.

Yes sir, I came to realize that Talking Rock was a wise man. And I felt right good toward Ma, too, since she didn't act riled at me either. 'Course Ma's a loving ma.

Hawkeye Hawkins came up on one of the black horses pulling the Carrekers' cow, and he and Goliath Dan un-hitched my team and led them down to the creek to water. Hawkeye later returned with good news. "Your beasts are fine, Jon-boy," he said, "except two of them whose hind legs got bloodied up some, which will heal in time."

That made me feel a whole lot better, and I was even happier when Hawkeye told me also the two wagons were only skint up in a few places, but nothing serious.

"Let's pitch camp right here for the night," Talking Rock said, and that pleased us all. We'd had enough excitement for one day, and after a little supper, I went straight to bed. And so did everyone else.

# CHAPTER THREE

## A Tavern Incident & Reaching the River Hi-wass'ee

Gunshots rang out and we jumped up from our plates of beans and cornbread to see what was happening. Two rough-looking fellows, bearded and wearing heavy boots, maybe drovers, came staggering down the road, apparently kicked out of the house of entertainment. They were powerful likkered up; I could smell it strong.

"And who might you folks be?" the bearded redhead asked, shuffling over in a tilt, looking Ma over up and down with a slow grin.

Chief Talking Rock spoke up quickly. "We're bringing these Virginians down to the Hi-wass'ee Valley mission. Mistress Merion here will be a new school teacher there and this is her son Jon. The rest of these folks also are going in to help out the missionaries already there."

"Wall," the red head said, "you'ns best hurry up and get your teachin' and preachin' done, 'cause the Cherokees ain't gon'a be around hyar much longer. Us Georgians is gon'a help 'em find a damn new home…way out west."

"Feller," Talking Rock said. "Watch your language before the lady."

"And who d'ye think you are, settin' the rules of eddiket around here? You look like a low down mixed-breed redskin to me."

I could see Talking Rock's neck turning crimson. He took a half step forward and with a smashing blow from his angry right fist, knocked the red head to the ground.

The man's drunken buddy shuffled up. "Now why'd you have to do that fer?" he whined.

"Get him away from here," Talking Rock said. "We don't need ignorant malcontents such as you two anywhere near the Cherokee Nation." The second fellow woke his partner with a few slaps to the face and they staggered off into the night.

"Sorry you were subjected to such rudeness, Mistress Rebecca," Talking Rock said.

"Thank you, sir," Ma said. After a pause, she added, "Tell me, Chief Talking Rock, when do you think we'll reach our destination?"

"We're awfully close, ma'am. Just hold tight till tomorrow."

"I wann'a take a dip, Dan!" Kindness Haughton screamed from the front seat of their wagon as we stopped at a little rise looking over the Hi-wass'ee River in western North Carolina.

"Lord, wife, you got to wade in every creek we pass," Goliath Dan roared. "We ain't got time; we need to get on down the road to the mission south of Brasstown, near the Georgee border."

"But this is the great River Hi-wass'ee, Dan," she pleaded. "Just let me stick my feet in for a few seconds."

"Oh, all right. I don't guess I see any harm in it if you don't, Talking Rock."

The chief nodded his okay with a smile and yelled:

"All right, folks, tie up your horses; we'll take a short break here to let you all check out the river. You're soon going to be seeing a lot of that stream when you get to your new home. Which, by the way, is just down the road apiece."

Kindness was the first one to reach the river's edge. "*Oooooooh, this water is cooooollllddd!* " she shrieked after sticking her right foot into the bold stream.

"You mighty right," Talking Rock replied. "Now if you want to test out some *really* cold water, Kindness, just go to one of our mountain springs. That, I might add, is where you can find the best drinking water, and, if you missionaries will pardon the expression, that's where the best corn recipe is made in these parts."

"Now wait just a minute, Chief Talking Rock! " Ma spoke up from the river bank: "You might as well know

now; we don't believe it's godly to partake of ardent spirits. So we don't want you to be tempting our believers."

Within minutes, all four families plus Talking Rock, Gilda, Hawkeye and Merlin were cavorting in the wild river's dancing waters. Goliath Dan's twin boys and the Carreker kids quickly found a deep place in which to swim. A leafy overhanging limb provided plenty of cover so they stripped naked and jumped in. Most of the men, including me, rolled up our pants to the knees and waded in.

"You all better be careful up there next to that bank!" Talking Rock boomed out. "There may be some water moccasins around there."

"Water moccasins?" I yelled, as I waded upstream with water nearly up to my knees.

"They're as mean and sneakin' a snake as I've ever known," Talking Rock said. "Even though they're fatter than a rattlesnake, they can swim faster than any dog and that's another thing, I'm going to tie up Goodness and Mercy 'cause water moccasins are bad on dogs. They hang up on tree limbs and dive down and strike like a bolt of lightning."

Goliath Dan, ignoring the warnings, kept on swimming after checking out the old beech tree that curved out over the river's deep spots. The rest of the crowd confined themselves to wading on the more shallow edge of the wide river.

As I walked down the river bed, I suddenly felt bites on my feet.

"*Something's biting my toes!*" I yelled. "*Are they water moc-*

*casins?"*

"Goodness no, Jon, those are minnows," Talking Rock replied. "You could see him if it was a snake. Those are baby trout and perch."

After I quit sloshing around, the stream became crystal clear, so clear I could look straight through to the bottom, like clear glass. "This river is teeming with fish!" I hollered again.

"Absolutely," Talking Rock said. "This country is fresh from the hand of God. You're coming into a territory that hasn't yet been spoiled by the white man . . . not much of it, at least, not up here in the mountains. These rivers and creeks, even the little branches, are swarming with bream and mountain trout and perch. There are enough fish right in here to feed an army."

"Are there many other species hereabouts?" Merlin asked.

"You mean any other kind of fish, Mister Merlin? The most extensive one that I haven't mentioned is the catfish."

"*Catfish?*" Merlin said. "I've never heard of such."

"That's what we Indians and mountain whites call that slick grayish fish right over there that's got all those strange bones sticking out from his head like whiskers on a cat's face."

"Well, I'll be," Ma said from the bank, smiling one of her rare smiles.

Against Talking Rock's warnings, Merlin and I wandered downstream. It was exciting walking in the fast moving water. I had my head down, looking at all the fish, thinking I should reach down and grab me a handful. When I looked up, I saw two fellows coming toward us in a canoe. Both were stripped down to loin skirts. Their brownish muscles glistened even in the shade and it was obvious they were Indians.

"We have some Indians here, Merlin!" I said.

Of a sudden, the pair ran their canoe into the bank and tied it to a sapling.

"Halloo," said the taller of the two, as he jumped out of the boat. "You must be the newcomers from Virginia. I'm Corn Silk, son of Su-ta'li and one of the mission linksters. And this is my friend, Spring Frog. Welcome to the Cherokee Nation."

"Thank you," Merlin said, shaking their arms and introducing me. "It's a pleasure to meet you both. I guess you know that all of our crowd are from Virginia except for me. I'm from Charleston in the South Carolina Low Country. I'll be one of your new ministers. You said you're a linkster, an interpreter?"

Before Corn Silk had a chance to answer, he sighted Talking Rock and yelled out to him and ran downstream and gave him a bear hug. That was the first time I'd ever seen two men hugging like that. It looked a little strange but I felt kind'a good about it, being such a wonderful demonstration of friendship.

"By golly, Corn Silk," Talking Rock said, "I'm mighty proud to lay eyes on you again. You too, Spring Frog." He draped his other arm over Spring Frog's shoulder.

"Merlin, these are my fishing buddies," the chief said.

After a pause, he declared, "Where have you been lately, Corn Silk?"

"Attending the Presbyterian School at Brainerd, up near Chat'a-noo'ga."

"Well good for you. You'll probably be going on to college in Connecticut, like young John Ridge and his cousin Buck Watie. We're mighty proud of you young scholars. You'll be running the Cherokee government one day when the old heads like Pathkiller and Major Ridge pass on."

"And how about you, Talking Rock?" Corn Silk asked.

"Gilda and I have been gone for almost two months now; we met these good folks up in Virginia. We've been serving as their guides and linksters."

"And as good a guide as there's ever been," Ma said, introducing herself. "Don't know how we'd have gotten here if it hadn't been for Chief Talking Rock and Gilda Goldenfeather."

"By the way, Corn Silk," Merlin said, "I've heard a lot about you, that you're the Number 1 linkster in the Cherokee Nation and a splendid ball player."

"Thank you, sir," he replied, smiling modestly. "But I'm afraid my ball-playing has gotten me into trouble with the head missionary. He hates the ball play."

Merlin changed the subject quickly, and said, "Let me ask you, Corn Silk, how far would you say we are from the mission?"

"Let's see, as the hawk flies, it must be no more than four miles. But the way the turnpike twists and turns, it'll be more like five or six miles. Even so, you should be there in less than an hour."

"That's exactly what Talking Rock told us just after we arrived here," Merlin said with a wink. "I just wanted to check on his accuracy."

"You just wait 'til I get you out hunting, Preacher Merlin," Talking Rock shot back with a wide grin. I'll get you so lost in the Nan'ta'ha-lee Mountains you'll never be able to find your way back home. That is unless a friendly Cherokee happens along and leads you back by the hand."

"Sometimes even Indians lose their bearings," Corn Silk laughed.

"I haven't seen an Indian yet who has ever got lost in the wild. We Indians have a natural navigating instinct. And we're mighty good at tracking, too. Most Indians can trail a bear for miles and miles. Same for tracking people and the very best at reading sign."

Talking Rock looked up at the sun that was hanging low on the western horizon and brought the visiting to an end.

"Let's load up, folks, it's time to get started on our last leg."

He invited Corn Silk and Spring Frog to load their canoe in one of the wagons and ride back with us.

"That would be wonderful," Corn Silk said. Spring Frog instead volunteered to run ahead to notify the community that the newcomers were on their way. "I can get there long before you do," he said, bouncing up and down on his moccasins.

"Very well, Spring Frog," Talking Rock replied. "You tell Preacher Paul we've got a bunch of hungry people and to lay on a good supper." Goliath Dan blew three times on his fox horn and Talking Rock yelled out, "WA - GON .. . HO!"

As our wagons creaked out from the little rise, I could see Spring Frog's legs pumping up and down as he melted into the green forest.

# CHAPTER FOUR

## The Arrival

It was pitch dark when we arrived, and long lines of young Cherokee students greeted us at the mission entrance. Holding candles and singing away, they were lined up on each side of the road. "What wonderful singing," Ma said as our wagons creaked by. Their hymns were in Cherokee but I recognized one by its tune, "Dove of Jesus, Descend on Us." And another:

*Lead, kindly light, amid the circling gloom*
*Lead me on,*
*The night is dark, and I am far from home,*
*Lead me on.*

Ma broke down and sobbed a bit and I guess I would have too if I hadn't been a man, 'cause my heart was crying inside. A man swinging a lantern met us when we reached the mission church and Talking Rock, who had gotten off Wagon 1, was standing there, too. Ma got off first and Talking Rock introduced her to the head missionary, Reverend Paul Proctor.

"Good evening, Mistress Merion," Reverend Proctor said. "Welcome to our mission. I hope you all had a good trip."

"We did indeed, sir, thanks to the guidance of Chief Talking Rock and Gilda Golden-feather, and we're mighty happy to finally be here." The head missionary expressed sadness about the untimely death of Reverend Merion in Virginia. "Spring Frog ran in just before you arrived," he said, "and brought us the sad news."

Ma then told him all about the circumstances of Pa's death and then introduced Reverend Merlin, the new missionary from Charleston.

After shaking Merlin's hand, Preacher Paul turned to me.

"And this must be your son."

"Yes, this is Little Jon. He was the driver of our wagon."

"My goodness, lad, that's amazing! How old are you?"

"Fourteen going on fifteen."

"You sure are tall for your age."

"He's growing up like a weed," Ma said. "He's almost as tall as his papa was."

I was mighty relieved that no mention was made about

my runaway wagon and horses that had run wildly down the Un-i'coi Gap.

Talking Rock turned over our horses and wagon to a black man whose head was crowned with a shock of curly white hair.

"Good evenin', Chief Talking Rock," he said. "Glad you be back safe and sound."

"It was a wonderful adventure, Jacob, but we're mighty happy to be back at home." It was shock, seeing a black man for the first time ever, and here in the Cherokee Nation of all places. I figured we'd find only Indians and a few whites here. Then I remembered hearing Gilda speak of the Negro Jacob while we were on the road.

"Years ago," Talking Rock told us later, "Jacob and Naomi fled from their abusive white master in Augusta and took up with us. We couldn't get along without them. Naomi runs the kitchen and Jacob does odd jobs. And, of course, they're devout members of our church."

We were directed to our cabin next door to the home of Talking Rock and Gilda. I was glad to learn also that Missionary Merlin was assigned a cabin nearby. Goliath Dan and family got a place near the grist mill and the Carrekers were taken to their new home next to the blacksmith shop.

We hadn't had a chance to turn around good before the young singers circled our cabin with their candles and started singing a new hymn. At the same time, Cherokee families began lining up at our front porch holding presents in their hands.

"What's going on?" Ma asked.

"This is what we call a pounding," Corn Silk said. "Members of our church are bearing gifts to help you get started here."

A Cherokee by the name of *Deer-in-the-Water* walked up with his family's gift. He spoke in Cherokee. Ma turned to Corn Silk.

"He says he wishes you a happy stay here and welcomes you to the Cherokee Nation. He is giving you a smoke-cured venison ham, along with a basket his wife made from river cane." The man shook hands with us and bowed politely as he moved back.

Before it was all done, our porch was filled with gifts. We could feel the sincere love of these Cherokees even though they were complete strangers. Ma wanted to say a word of thanks and Corn Silk got the crowd's attention. The mission grounds turned so quiet only the popping of the torches out front could be heard.

"Thank you all, good people, for your wonderful welcome and for your kind gifts," Ma said. "We are so proud to join you here and we pray our friendship will last for years to come. My only regret is that my husband, who died on our trip, wasn't here to witness your marvelous reception and warm welcome. Thank you one and all."

Well sir, after that, the singers and the candles and torches faded away, one by one, into the dark. Preacher Paul then invited us to join him and his staff for supper. The cook, the black lady Naomi, Jacob's wife, had laid out a long table loaded with venison ham and biscuits and butter, plus potatoes and milk—everything produced right there on the mission farm, they told us.

After Preacher Paul said grace, I dug into the vittles, especially the biscuits and butter and pure sourwood honey. How wonderful! I made a pig of myself and I noticed Talking Rock watching me with pure amusement. After supper, an Indian with a shock of bushy red hair—Preacher Paul introduced him as Reverend Bushyred, "one of the great Cherokee exhorters"—arose to end our day with a word of prayer. I was glad he spoke partly in English; it was a powerful prayer and he grunted every time he came to a pause. His voice roared loud and then he'd go into a whisper. I'd never heard any praying like that before. Then it was all over.

I suddenly felt at home here in the heart of the Cherokee country. Ma said she felt the same way. But I didn't tell her that I had heard that the Cherokee Nation was under siege from nearby states and even the American president, who were said to be eager to remove the Cherokees to a territory far out west called Ark-can'saw, beyond what they called "the mother of all rivers."

Ma didn't get much sleep that first night, even though we were plumb tuckered out from the trip. She told me she tossed and turned all night long.

As for me, I slept like a bear hibernating in the dark of winter as Talking Rock would tell it. And my first night in the Indian country was taken up with a dream of going on a bear hunt. Talking Rock was in the lead, of course. Actually his hound dog Goodness was up front along with Mercy, the Indian cur, and yours truly had the honor of heading up the rear. The dogs led us right up to a rhododendron slick near a mountain bald. I'd heard tell how the banks of evergreen bushes and blooming green laurels were just about jungles, and now I saw for myself.

I could tell from the dogs' barking, plus some strange smells, that we were closing in on Mister Bear. Talking Rock stopped short and held up his hand. Then we threaded our way through another thicket of mountain honeysuckles and came onto a monstrous pile of chestnut leaves, piled up higher than my head.

Of a sudden, the dogs began barking at the top of their lungs. Before Talking Rock could swing his gun into shooting position, that bear came tearing out of the leaf pile. Boy was he big—tall as a sapling—and fat, black and furry. But he had a friendly face and a big wide grin! Quicklike, he stood up on his hind legs and waved his arms like he was leading a band. Before I knew it, the bear walked up and gave me a hug and kissed me on my right cheek. Then, quickly, he whirled around and dropped down on the ground and curled up into a monstrous black ball. That's the honest God truth, according to my dream! Then he started rolling, just like a flour barrel, and he rolled and rolled and rolled, right on down the side of the mountain and came out at a branch where he flattened out on all fours and jumped up and ran like a scalded dog, disappearing into the laurels. We just stood up there on that mountain top with our mouths gaping wide open.

All in all, it was a right powerful dream, better than any I'd ever dreamt before, although at the winding up of the dream, Talking Rock spoke of how sick he was cause we didn't bring home any "bar meat." On the other hand, I had become awfully curious about the romantic old bear that had turned acrobat and rolled down the hill like a ball!

The next morning, Ma said the ingredients for the dream came straight from my wild imagination, bolstered by Talking Rock's bear-hunting tales that had got stored up in my noggin.

So I woke up in a feisty frame, and I didn't calm down good 'til Ma cooked us up some ham and eggs and hominy grits along with biscuits that gave my stomach divine contentment. 'Specially after she gave me a cup of coffee plus a second cup to make coffee soakee.

I was eager to get out and look over this end of the Cherokee Nation. Talking Rock promised me he would give us a grand tour soon. I couldn't wait, but one thing had me worried. Talking Rock told me we're only a few miles from the Georgee line.

# CHAPTER FIVE

## A Heaven on Earth

I was lucky that I didn't have to go to school right off, and it was wonderful the next morning to run smack dab into Talking Rock near our cabin. Naturally, I recalled to him my crazy dream again, the one in which the bear hugged and kissed me before he rolled down the hill and out of sight.

The chief squatted down on the ground next to me and we had us a nice little talk about bear hunting. (It's amazing, by the way, how Indians like Talking Rock can squat down on their haunches like a grasshopper for hours on end, as if on a rocking chair.)

"Now Jon Boy," he says, holding up his hunting knife and inspecting the blade, "there's only one thing wrong with that dream of yours. You must learn that if you manage to track a bear all that way up to his den, that you must bring him back dead or alive. That is, if he doesn't climb a tree and defecate on you and blind you so you can't see to shoot him. That happened to me one time, back in my younger years."

I concluded that the chief—the grandson of a Cherokee grandmother and a Scottish born trader grandfather—was educated in his own way with a special vocabulary to match. Who would ever have imagined that he would use such a word as defecate? I realized, of course, he was merely avoiding using that other word because Ma was nearby.

I knew right off after a lengthy visit with the chief that this wild valley was going to be lots of fun, although I soon came to the conclusion that there were many more mountains around here than valleys and that there were no towns at all. Mostly little settlements, or as local whites call them, *settlemints*. Ours, near Persimmon Creek, is the biggest village of the lot and we have only something like twelve or so families living here, according to Gilda Golden-feather, plus the fifty or so scholars who are boarding at the school, and the dozen or so teachers and mission people.

But I soon got the feeling that this magnificent valley was a true heaven on earth, situated as it is on a delightful knoll overlooking the Persimmon Creek Valley and with magnificent bottom lands of corn, beans and squash lined up in long rows stretching far into the distance toward the grand Hi-wass'ee River. Plus a nice patch of sorghum cane, from which the scholars will be chopping down and squeezing into juice for boiling in a big hot vat that will result into delicious sorghum syrup. Or so says the chief.

Looking over to the west I was amazed at how the hills stretched on up to the first mountain. That leads to another mountain, higher and higher piled on top of one another and right on up to the top of what I was told were the O-co'ee, Snowbird and Un-i'coi ranges. On the eastern side, the same scenery extends to the gorgeous Nan-ta'ha'lee mountains, I was told.

"Our Indians," Talking Rock told me, "consider the mountain ranges ancient spirits, looking down on us with love and affection."

I created in my mind a silent prayer to my late father:

*"Pa, I'm so sorry you didn't get down here to see this part of our world in all its magnificence; you would've loved it. God rest your soul.—Your son Jon."*

A few days after we arrived here in this end of the Cherokee nation, I decided, just for the fun of it, to tease the young chief a little.

"Talking Rock," I asked, "are there much fauna around here?"

"I guess you might say there is," he replied.

"How bout the flora?"

"What are you talking about boy?" he replied. Then he saw my sly grin and realized I'd been teasing him. He slapped me real sharp on the shoulder and said with a smile, "You whippersnapper you!"

My shoulder smarted quite a while after that and I quickly found out that the chief knew a whole lot more about those subjects than I ever would. After all, he had been living the outdoor life ever since he was a kid.

"Just wait'll I get you out bear hunting, young feller," he said, "and I'll show you a thing or two about fauna. Black bears are out there by the hundreds all across our Nan-ta'hal'ee and Snowbird Mountains."

I immediately tried to get back in his good graces and asked, "Is it true, Talking Rock, that a Cherokee will pray for an animal's soul before he pulls the trigger?"

"That's the absolute truth, boy, and we're mighty thankful to the creatures in the forest—particularly the bears and the deer—for giving up their lives so we can have enough venison and bear meat to feed our families through the year. That bear meat, by the way, provides important cooking oil and oil for our lamps, besides giving us some awful good eatin'. And don't ever forget that a bear skin makes the warmest coat a person could ever hope to wear in the freezing months of winter."

Talking Rock was proving to be a pure curiosity. No

sooner had he finished telling me stories about bears than he got into the subject of trees.

"You see that line of timber over yonder?" he said, pointing to a grove to the south of the mission church. "What kind of tree do you reckon is that real tall one in front?"

"I'm afraid I'm right ignorant about that one, sir," I confessed.

"Well, Jon, that's a chestnut, the greatest breed of timber ever to grace our land. Not only do those trees feed our bears and other animals like deer, squirrels and even wild turkeys with its juicy mast, chestnut's the best wood that you could imagine, being easy to cut and yet long lasting when split out for our puncheon floors."

"And moreover," he said, "chestnut wood delivers ferocious flames in a fireplace. One of our old timers says he wants to be buried in a chestnut coffin so he can go through hell a'poppin'!"

"Mast?" I asked. That's a word I've never heard of before.

"You never heard tell of mast?" he said. "You should ask the bears and the other animals about mast. That's what they gobble up for breakfast, dinner and supper, particularly in the fall of the year. Walnuts and chestnuts and hickory nuts and acorns and chinquapins and even hazelnuts. That's how our animals fatten up for the cold winter months when some of 'em crawl into hollowed out logs and go to sleep until springtime."

And during the late summer months, he told me that, "the animals feast on wild muscadines and persimmons and fox grapes and 'possum grapes. All part of what we call the forest mast, a cornucopia of edible goodies thanks to the benevolence of the Lord above.

"'Course now," he continued, "Our Indians harvest their share of those nuts and fruits, too. We're awful gifted at preserving apples and peaches, slicing them up and drying them in the sun. Same for pumpkins that we cut into spirals and hang out to dry. Then there are leather britches, the snap beans that we string up to dry in the summer sunshine.

Those dried pumpkins and leather britches come in real handy in the dead of winter, like February, when our cupboards are getting bare. That's when we bring down the bags of dried leather britches from the loft, add a little water in the pot along with a chunk of salted bear meat or pork and boil up a delicious dish of string beans. Cook 'em slow all day in the fireplace."

"And you call those beans 'leather britches'?"

"Yes. They got named that when our people noticed that when they used a big needle and thread to hang the string beans out on to dry, the beans shriveled up in the hot sun, leaving them looking like a pair of beat up britches."

Well sir, I just sat there and gazed at Talking Rock with more admiration than ever. Like I said, he was proving to be a real curiosity and as Ma called him a "Rock of Gibraltar," being full of first hand knowledge about the Cherokee people, their history and environment.

It grieved me that I'd tried to tease him. I went to my knees in prayer that night, asking God's forgiveness for my awful rudeness and vowing to never let it happen again.

Like I said, I felt fortunate I didn't have to go to school right off. That gave me a chance to wander around some more with the chief. He was on call to go down to the grist mill and he invited me to tag along. Ma was glad to get shed of me, being as she was busy getting our cabin aired out.

I quickly learned that I'd have to move extra fast to keep up. The chief takes long strides, like Pa did. Every time he'd take a step, I'd have to run a couple.

We went down a trail through the woods and came to Persimmon Creek. "It's right peaceable today," he said, "but you should see her when she gets angry, right after a thunderstorm. That creek can turn mean in a hurry and slosh way over her banks just like that," snapping his fingers.

The chief suddenly flopped down flat on his belly on the water's edge and slurped up water like a dog. I decided I'd do the same.

"That's awful sweet water," he said, wiping his mouth with the back of his hand.

"Shore is," I replied, after slurping up my share, and using one of his favorite sayings.

We took off our shoes and waded barefoot across the creek. The frigid water nearly froze my tender feet.

"It's so cold," I cried.

"You'll get used to it after a while, boy."

Talking Rock told me he would give me and some of the others a grand tour in the morning that he'd been promising, including a visit with Oak Tree, the great full-blood.

I couldn't wait.

# CHAPTER SIX

## Meeting Little Fox & Oak Tree

"Hal-lo, Jon-boy," Oak Tree said, grabbing my right arm with a 'Cherokee arm shake.' It felt like he was about to lift me off the ground. He had dark eyes and a dark coppery skin, sure signs of a full-blood, plus a big smile, and I was told he had a heart of gold.

"Oak Tree lives right here near the grist mill," Talking Rock said. "His job is keeping the mill going day in and day out. He's not acquainted with many English words but he's picked up quite a few phrases and he's a wonder at sign language."

Oak Tree's new boss, Goliath Dan Haughton, the wheel-wright, was already on the job and eagerly led us across the trail to the mill. The weathered frame structure—built on heavy oak stilts—was situated right behind the dam and the huge water wheel. Dan took us up some stone steps where we got a nice view of the dam and lake. But he was paying little attention to the scenery. He was concentrating on the big water wheel just below the dam.

"This wheel," Dan declared, "powers the turning of the heavy mill stone below and that grinds the shelled corn into meal."

"*Turn it on, Oak!*" Goliath Dan said, raising his voice and gesturing with his right hand in a spinning motion. Oak Tree scrambled to pull a handle engaging a clutch. Suddenly a stream of water shot onto the big wheel, filling the slats and forcing the wheel to start turning, squeaking slowly at first, and then building up to a steady noise that took on a load pulse beat of its own.

"*Holy damn!*" Dan yelled, breaking into a jig.

"Watch it, Dan," Talking Rock yelled. "This a religious community; remember?"

"Sorry. Let me start all over," he said. "*Jumping Jehosephats!*"

It was good that he corrected himself because we saw Missionary Merlin and Preacher Paul coming our way down the trail to the mill along with Corn Silk, the linkster.

"*Start the stone!*" Dan yelled, forgetting to use sign language. Oak Tree pulled another lever, causing the huge granite mill stone on top to start turning. I noticed that the second stone underneath remained locked in place. The building started shaking and thundering and the noise of the rotating stone added to the racket that shook the entire frame building.

"*Oak, run corn through!*" Dan yelled. The Indian pulled another lever, and a stream of shelled corn started pouring into the center of the rotating rock. Of a sudden, I could see steaming white meal shooting out of the edge of the millstone and going into a wooden box.

Dan picked up a slick pine paddle, slipped his thumb and fingers through the cutout holes and scooped up a pile of the fresh meal from the box. It gave off a hot, sweet smell. He wet his stubby left index finger, stuck it into the meal and put it to his tongue.

"That'll sure make some mighty fine corn bread," he hollered.

We turned to see Merlin walking up with Corn Silk and Preacher Paul. Dan reached out his hand to the head missionary and spoke in a loud voice so he could be heard over the noise.

"Good morning, sir. I'm Goliath Dan Haughton, your new wheelwright. I guess I'll be running this mill in the future for you folks, along with Oak Tree, of course. I'm happy the mill's running mighty fine today."

"I can see you're in your element, Mister Haughton," Preacher Paul replied.

"Sir," Dan said, "get a little taste of this." He brought up a fresh scoop of ground meal and poured it into the head missionary's left palm.

"Tastes fine," he replied after sticking his tongue to a small sample. "Looks like we'll have bread for the winter.

Praise the Lord."

Preacher Paul dismissed himself and Dan took Merlin on a tour of the place, including the dam, lake and spillway. Naturally, I trailed along every step of the way. We climbed the rock steps on the back side of the dam and paused at the top. It was an awesome view. The crystal clear reservoir reflected the noontime sun and we noticed two Cherokees out fishing.

"Talking Rock," Dan said, "This dam looks awful narrow, maybe only sixty feet across, what you could call the 'Eye of the Needle.' It's a perfect spot to capture water and generate power. But I'm afraid that in a heavy storm this dirt dam could suffer a lot of erosion. It needs to be shored up soon with rocks."

"You're right," Talking Rock said with a frown, as he made a note to himself.

Later on, Talking Rock took us around the settlement and introduced us to a bunch of folks, including Oak Tree's beautiful wife Laugh'in-gal, who stands two hands taller than Oak Tree and whose luxurious black hair extends way down her back.

The chief then led us a good way to the cabin of the widow Su-ta'li and her sons Corn Silk and his younger brother, *Little Fox*. The younger boy looked to be about my age and we hit it right off. I was happy that he spoke our language. Said he learned it from his Pa, a mixed-blood Cherokee, who had died, I was sorry to hear, in the 1814 Battle of Horseshoe Bend. "He was fighting with the Cherokee Regiment in the war against the Upper Creek Red Sticks," the boy said.

"I think I'm going to like it here," I told Ma that night.

"Is that a fact now?"

"Yes, ma'am; I met an Indian boy today who's going to teach me to fish and swim and spy on the wild animals, and maybe even help me learn to speak Cherokee."

"And who might that be, pray tell?"

"His name is Little Fox. He's the son of the widow Su-ta'li and is the Corn Silk's brother."

"I'd like to know more about this Little Fox," Ma said. "I'm not sure that you're ready to be going out in these woods around here with the Indians just yet. You've heard Talking Rock tell about all the varmints that populate the wilds, including bears, wolves, rattlers and I don't know what all."

"Little Fox says they're not to be feared," I said, "that most creatures are right friendly. He even gives nice rub-downs to the snakes and frogs he captures. He claims they love it."

"What kind of snakes, Jon?"

"Not the mean ones like rattlers, but the chicken snakes, the green snakes and the rat snakes."

"Well, I'm not going to feel comfortable with you out there roaming around with an Indian chasing down snakes and frogs."

"Don't be hasty, Ma. Little Fox might be a good companion. Maybe he can teach me some of the Indian ways that would come in handy around here."

Ma turned silent and drew unto herself. I could understand her feelings. She still carried a heaviness in her heart without having Pa around. And I could tell she didn't want me running loose outdoors, remembering the likes of the panther that prowled around our camp that night we spent in East Tenn-a'see.

The next day, I told Ma I had run into Little Fox again. "And while I was there, he picked up a green snake and let him curl around his arm just as pretty as you please. He talked to him and kissed him."

I knew right off that I shouldn't have told her that.

"He kisses snakes? Dear Lord in Heaven, Little Jon, don't tell me my son is taking up with a snake-kissing aborigine."

"Talking Rock says Little Fox would be a good buddy for me. Like I said yesterday, he can teach me many of the Indian tricks."

"We'll see," Ma said, sounding awfully unconvinced. I

was sorry she didn't see it my way, but I figured I could get Talking Rock and Merlin to speak some words of support. I felt right certain that they could bring Ma around, although it might take another week or so.

# CHAPTER SEVEN

## The Secret Place

Jacob rang the school bell and I walked in and took my seat on the half log next to Little Fox. But try as I might, I couldn't keep my mind on anything other than our secret place. It's located on a small creek leading into Persimmon Creek and it belongs to Fox and me. Well, it was Little Fox's to begin with since he discovered it. But he gave me halvers on it when he took me in for the first time, and now we own it equal, him and me, fair and square. Fact is, nobody else knows about it but us, so I guess that means it can't be anybody else's.

Sitting there in Mistress Comfort Carreker's class, waiting for my math assignment, I recalled that first day when Little Fox revealed the hideaway to me and decided to take me in as his partner. Like I mentioned earlier, his daddy, Jim Eagle, had taught him to speak English and that made it easy for us to become good friends from the start. And like I said, he agreed to teach me to speak Cherokee.

Before Fox took me to the secret place after school the day before, we walked down to the creek to go fishing. He told me he was going to show me how to fish the Cherokee way.

"This is our fish trap, a rock wall fishing weir," he said, walking out into the creek's cold waters. What he had was a line of rocks two feet high coming out from each bank, going down stream in the shape of a "V." I helped him bring in some more rocks to pile up there at the tip of the "V."

After we got the trap in place, and the water started rising behind the rocks, Fox sent me upstream. "When I give you the signal," he said, "I want you to yell and pop your hands and head the fish downstream." He took two baskets to the end of the dam's "V" point and lowered his head and whispered something, with his head bowed. Then he raised up and whistled for me to start up my noisemaking.

Well sir, my eyes double-danced at the sight of what happened next. When I yelled and clapped, the fish started swimming straight toward the trap. Fox commenced scooping 'em into his baskets. Pretty soon we had us a good mess of trout and bream, some bigger than Hawkeye's hand, plus a couple of cats and two or three Ku'sa bass. I knew we were in for some good eating.

We could've caught us a lot more, but Fox soon put a

stop to it, saying there was no need to kill more fish than necessary. He even tossed the cats, the Ku'sa bass and a few bream back into the creek below the dam. He pulled out some rocks to let the water run free, and said, "Get going, fellows, and stay away from rock dams in the future." Just like that.

"Our Yo'wah God," Fox said, "wants us to harvest ever bit of nature's food that we need, but never to rob fish or animals from Mother Earth's rivers or forests just for the fun of it."

Then it came clear to me why Fox was whispering before he started the fish catch. I'd heard tell of Indians praying before shooting animals. Later I asked him about it and he said that he was raising up a prayer asking the Creator God's forgiveness for taking the lives of the fish he'd be catching. In other words, an unspoken prayer.

I told him that I knew all about unspoken prayers, because I had sent several up to our own Creator God many a time, 'specially on that frightful afternoon when our wagon went plunging out of control down this end of the Un-i'coi Gap. "I got so scared," I said, "I got to praying out-loud prayers."

With our fishing being over, Little Fox got me to help him knock down a few more of the rocks through the middle of the dam so the water could run free and the fish could swim whichever way they wanted, upstream or downstream or stay where they were.

When we started home, Fox said, "I want to show you something, Jon." He led me up a path to another creek maybe 200 yards away, but running in the same direction as Persimmon Creek.

Little Fox veered sharp left around a cane thicket and then straight into a heavy patch of rhododendrons and huckleberries. It took us a while picking our way through and I got cut up a little, mostly on account of the blackberry briars and wild grape vines flopping back and slapping me on the face.

Next we had to fight our way through a wall of wisteria vines and Virginia creepers that dipped down from low hanging beech trees. Finally he pulled back a wall of the vines, opening a little door. We crawled in on all fours and came smack dab into his secret hideaway!

I was plumb startled at the sight. We were inside what looked like a big room with walls of vines and flowers and with mockingbirds and flying squirrels flittin' all around. The ceiling was like a giant parasol with blooming honeysuckle vines stretching over the branch from bank to bank. The other end was covered with what looked like a wild grape arbor of possum grapes and fox grape vines plus elderberries. "In the fall," he said, "all a body has to do is reach up and pluck some of those grapes to eat. I love it when they bleed sweet juice down my arms when I'm eating them."

Yes sir-ree, Little Fox's hideaway was something to see—
a sure enough marvel. Like I said, the creek runs parallel to
Persimmon Creek and forms most of the hideaway's floor,
flowing right through the middle, quiet and serene, over
slick flat rocks, and there at the curve I could see a stretch
of water that formed a nice little pond.

It almost took my breath away and Little Fox could see
I was stunned by it all.

I followed him down to a little beach of white sand that
had washed in onto one side of the stream. On the other
side was a boulder that stuck out over the water. Down below, the water was deeper than my head! We stood without
saying anything for a while, just enjoying the scene.

"Glory be, Fox," I said, breaking the silence, "how in the
devil did you find this place?"

"It was back before you and your crowd came down
from Virginia. I was floating down the creek in my canoe
when the water was up, but I couldn't get through the wall
of vines that blocked me off.

"I guess I could have swam under, but instead, I tied
up my boat and walked and walked and circled around
through the woods for a long time until I was able to pick
my way through from the other side. That's when I cut my
door through with my hunting knife. I've been back here
many times since then, particularly when I wanted to get
off and sit by myself and think about things for a spell."

I could've hugged Little Fox right then and there if I'd a
known him a little better, such a thrill it was to me. Except
I'd never seen the men folks in our family ever hug any-

body. Except Pa put his arm on Ma's shoulder one time.

I can hardly believe it, but it seems like Little Fox and I have known one another forever. We race down to our hideaway every day after school and plot our future and ponder our past. As I mentioned earlier I had learned that his Pa, Big Fox, was killed in that Battle of Horseshoe Bend down on the River Ta-la'poo'sa. He was fighting with the Cherokee warriors against the "Red Stick" Creek Indian rebels who'd been killing off mixed-breed Creek chiefs who'd become friendly with their new American neighbors moving in.

"They were called Red Sticks because they carried clubs painted blood red, the color of war," Little Fox said, adding that they were identified with the Upper Creeks, 'cause they had a trail, the Upper Creek Path, that crossed over to the west side of the great Chatt'a-hooch'ee River from the east side.

"Sometime I'd love to visit the Cherokee chief White Path over in El'i-ja," Fox said. "He fought with my father at the '*To-ho'pe-k* bend of the river' it was called."

When he grows up, Fox told me, he hopes to travel down to the spot down there where his pa is buried.

Later I went with Fox to his cabin where he lives with his mother Su-ta'li and his brother Corn Silk. Their place sits on a little rise up way up on Persimmon Creek. She makes baskets out of the sweet grass and river canes and trades them for coffee to trader Murphy who sends the baskets down to Augusta on the backs of his horses.

Since we've become friends, Fox and I have held some deep discussions at our place like, "Where did we all come from when we were born?" And, "Where did the sun and the moon and the stars come from?"

"All of those, particularly the sun and moon, were sacred to us when I was growing up here in this valley," Fox said. "So were the waterways which all have their own spirits just like all the animals in the forest!"

That was a startling revelation to me, but Fox said it had been told to him by the Cherokee conjurer priests when he was growing up and that he had come to have a powerful belief in such.

'Course I begged to differ with Little Fox about spirits, in particular animal spirits. I told him that our God was far away but also was close at hand, being always in our minds and hearts.

"I can raise up a prayer to our Lord at any time I wish," I said. "Naturally you have to be in the right frame of mind to listen to what God says in reply. Sometimes his reply can take a while and his answer may come to you as a complete surprise in an unusual way or maybe months later."

"You mean he actually answers you when you pray?"

"Sure," I said. "Our God's son Christ came to earth years and years ago in the form of a human being just like us.

That's why they call us Christians. Our religion is named for Christ who, after being slain on the cross, came back to life and went to Heaven to be with God, his Father."

"I think I've heard about that man," Fox said. "Is he the one they nailed onto a dead tree where he was stabbed and bled to death and then three days after he was put into a rock tomb, he sprung back to life and later rose to heaven?"

"*Yes, that's right!*" I said and I congratulated Fox on his remembering all that. "We believe it to be true."

But Little Fox said he wasn't yet ready to place much store in somebody like that.

Little Fox and I soon got where we were spending nearly ever day at our secret place after school, and we made a blood oath that we would never tell anyone about it, not even Talking Rock or my ma. We wrote down our secret bond, ending with the words, "*Cross my heart and hope to die.*"

We love to lie on the water's edge and watch the animals walk up to drink out of the creek—the beavers and squirrels and raccoons. Early of an evening, the ring-tailed raccoons, cute little fellers, come up and sit on their hind legs and eat most anything you lay out there for them, shaking it clean. They'll look you straight in the eye and act just as natural as you please.

"Each animal has his own spirit about him," Fox said, "and was put on earth by the Great Spirit, just as our Cherokee ancestors were placed here in these very mountains by our Creator God years and years ago."

We had a bunch of things to talk about and many was the time we'd come out from our secret place feeling as if we had been in touch with the Great Spirit of the world, his and mine.

Leaving our place through the tunnel, we would shut the vine door back and would take a different route across the huckleberries and the cane brake. We didn't want to set up a regular path and leave sign. Otherwise the whole settlement would find out. Of course, it's a well-known fact that Indians are good at reading sign in the woods.

Fox and I came up with our own special whistles to signal one another. Mine is two sharp toots at a high pitch. When Little Fox hears it, he knows that I'll meet him at the hideout. He answers with his whistle—a short blast at a low pitch followed by a long whistle that sweeps to a high note on a shrill rise.

I marveled at Little Fox's whistling skill. "You sound just like a whippoorwill," I told him one day. That pleased him mightily; I learned that he liked whippoorwills about as much as mockingbirds and hummingbirds.

"Our word for whippoorwill is *Wa-gu'li*," he replied.

"*Wa-gu'li?*" I yelled, and it struck me like a candle lighting up in my head.

"I think I'll call you Wa-gu'li," I said. "Wa-gu'li, the boy who whistles like a whippoorwill! "

"You look to me like a Wa-gu'li," I continued, "excepting you don't have wings. But Wa-gu'li will make you a marvelous name even so."

Fox studied the ground a bit and then I noticed the corners of his mouth turning up a little when he looked me in the eye. He told me the missionaries give Christian names to Cherokees when they're baptized, like Matthew and John and Mary and Ruth.

"Like my Aunt Louise," he said. "She's named for a widow's mite Baptist lady in Charleston, a Mrs. Louise Simpson, who sends money to the mission cause from time to time."

"I bet none of them have ever got named for a bird! " I laughed.

"Well, no they haven't, come to think about it."

I started spreading the word about Fox's new name and Merlin and Hawkeye and even Talking Rock helped me talk it up all around. Some of the Cherokee young folks started whistling and waving their arms like a bird when passing Wa-gu'li. It puffed him up real good. Which I enjoyed a whole heap.

One day Gu'li got to thinking and decided that instead of calling me Jon, he'd call me by the Cherokee word for John—T'san.

"Actually, we'll call you *T'san-us'di*," Fox said. "That

stands for Little John."

And before you know it, the new name caught in our village. It got to where nobody much called me Jon anymore. Even Goliath Dan and Comfort Carreker started calling me T'san-us'di, and also Oak Tree and Laugh-in'gal.

In the meanwhile, Wa-gu'li's whippoorwill whistling got better and better. All manner of birds started flying around him, in particular mockingbirds and bluebirds, and sometimes hummingbirds, all trying to find out where the bird sounds were coming from.

Cherokee boys and girls across the valley started asking Gu'li and me to teach them to make bird calls like that, which we were happy to do.

# CHAPTER EIGHT

## Getting to Know Chief Talking Rock

"It's *Nunyu-gun'wani'ski*," Gu'li said, "*The Rock That Talks*. That's Talking Rock's name in Cherokee."

"Sure is a mouthful," I said, "but it's a perfect name for sure."

Our friendship with Talking Rock began in Virginia a month and a half ago. As I mentioned before, the young chief and his wife had arrived on their black horses at our camp just after we had laid my father to rest there in the Virginia wilds.

Their arrival helped get us through that sad period in our lives and they did a wonderful job getting us down through East Tenn-a'see and on to the decrepit U-ni'coi turnpike, such as it was, that led us here to Hi-wass'ee.

I connected with their dogs right away. The one they called Goodness was a big-eared hound dog and the other one, Mercy, was a cute little Indian cur.

I well remember our stop at the top end of of East Tenn-a'see where we camped out near the South Fork of the Holston River. When I got up early that morning and walked out to the campfire, the chief offered me a strong smelling cup of coffee, roasted from beans he'd just ground.

"Thank you, sir. I'd love to have a cup if I can turn it into coffee-soakee.

"Coffee soakee?" he asked, looking up with a grin.

"Yes sir. I soak a biscuit in cup of coffee of a morning and spoon it out. It's a delicious way to start one's day."

"Well now, boy," he said to me, "we gon'a have to get you started on drinking coffee straight up. By the way, Jon, what age be you now?"

"Just turned fourteen, sir."

"My Goodness, lad. You sure are a sizable fellow for your age. Now that your Pa is gone, if you'd like, I'll be happy to help you get along when we get down to the Cherokee country."

I told him I would appreciate his help a whole heap and asked how I could accomplish "growing up," as he called it, being as I am still a runt of a boy.

"First off, Jon, don't consider yourself a runt," he said. "You are filling out nicely and you're a fine looking lad to boot. So don't sell yourself short. To help you out, I'd like for you to start riding with me up on the front seat of our wagon."

"That would be wonderful, sir," I said. "I would love that!"

"And for 'growing up starters, I would advise you to take on every chore you can that'll help your ma, like bringing in the water from the spring, chopping up the fire wood, and so forth. Just make yourself useful in every way possible."

"Could I help mistress Gilda right now?" I asked.

"You sure can, young feller," Gilda spoke up as she came out of the wagon heisting a hunk of salted side meat. "How 'bout fetching me some dead limbs so we can hot up our skillet and re-hot the coffee pot?" She was tickled to death when I came back with my arms loaded, 'specially when she saw the two big knots of fat litard wood that I'd placed on top.

"Wonderful, Jon-Boy," she said. "That'll shore give us the heat and fast too."

The early morning breakfast out there in the Tenn-a'see wilds—scrambled eggs, bacon and cornbread plus a cup of coffee soakee—quickly silenced the growling of my poor stomach. 'Course I had to soak corn pones into the coffee that day, instead of biscuits, but I didn't mind, since I knew it wouldn't be long before Ma would be cooking up plenty of biscuits once we reach Hi-wass'ee.

"Boy, that's a beautiful line of blue mountains over there on the left," I said as we rolled down the dirt trail.

"That's the Blue Ridge Mountain range," Talking Rock

said. "We'll be following those mountains for a hundred miles." Then he gave me a little history lesson of his people and their Cherokee nation.

"Jon, our Cherokees for thousands of years had owned and resided in hundreds of villages in those foothills and up the river valleys coming into the Tenn-a'see River. That is until the British at first burned our people out of their humble cabins down near the head of the Savannah River, and even cut down their livelihood, their young corn. But worst of all, a few years later, North Carolinian speculators near about stole most of our land along here as well as our hunting grounds in Middle Tenn-a'see and Kentuck."

"That must have been an awful time for your people," I said.

"Sure was, Jon-Boy." he replied. "It was a sad time."

Suddenly, taking a break from thinking about the dark days of the past, Talking Rock turned to me and said, "Here, Jon, take over the reins."

I straightened up quick like and took the handoff. Then I popped the leather on the horses pretty good. "Hold on now boy, not so fast!" he said. "Don't spank 'em hard when they're going good like now. Be gentle with them. That's how you win their confidence."

I liked Chief Talking Rock from the beginning and I think he took a liking to me, too. He stood tall and gangly like Pa, with a wide, friendly face. And he sure had the

Indian look to him; his skin gleamed like a sheet of copper in the sunlight and his jet black hair hung down straight and slick. I gathered he must keep his hair slicked up by slathering on bear oil like I'd heard most Indians do.

Later on, Ma came up with a thought. "The chief likely possesses some Scottish blood in him also," she said, "since he speaks with a quaint sort of English and most always has a fun-loving gleam in his blue eyes."

The next day we learned from Gilda that Talking Rock's grandpa was indeed a Scot straight out of Scotland, a trader to the Indians back in the olden days. And I learned the chief's father—who also married a Cherokee lass—followed in his dad's footsteps as a trading post operator at Tus-qui'ti located near our future home. "Thus I'm a thoroughbred mixed-breed Cherokee," he told me.

Later I told Ma, "you surely must possess second sight."

"Second sight?"

"Don't you know? That gives a person the ability to size up somebody at the very first glance. That's how you knew right off that Talking Rock was a Scot as well as a Cherokee!"

In the latter days of our trip down through East Tenn-a'see I well remember how the chief talked me into taking over the driver's seat of Wagon number 3. Rob Roarty had suffered an injury to his right wrist. "He won't be able to drive his team for the rest of our trip," Talking Rock told me.

"I'm sorry to hear that."

"Jon-Boy," he said, "You're a fast learner and even though you're a mite young, I'm convinced you can handle one of these wagons and the team of horses as well as most grownups. So I want you to take over as driver of wagon 3."

He must have noticed the shock on my face since my mouth was hanging wide open and my eyes were bulging out big. "*Unbelievable*," I thought to myself. He wants me, a youngster not yet dried behind the ears, as they say, to drive one of these four-horse teams? Surely he must be joshing.

"You're getting right stout, boy, and you can do it."

That bucked up my confidence somewhat, but I continued to wonder what would happen if my four big horses should run away with me and go in a different direction than they ought.

"I'll be leading off in the first wagon, as usual," the chief said, "and Goliath Dan will be following in number 2 with Conrad Carreker bringing up the rear directly behind you in number 4."

"*Chief Talking Rock*," I said, looking him straight in the eye, "*are you truly sure you want me to do this?*"

"Of course I do, Jon-Boy. I've asked Conrad Carreker to keep a special watch on you for a while since he'll be tailing you in wagon 4. And Rob Roarty—though he's handicapped—will be sitting with you at the front bench to give you advice should you need it."

I was still a bit shaky about the prospect.

"Just remember this," he told me. "Be kind to your horses, but be firm. That's the secret to handling the animals."

"Thank you, sir," I said, "I'll do my best." That's about all I could think to say since I was still in a state of shock.

As I climbed up into the left hand seat and was getting a feel for wagon's reins and horses, the chief walked up and pressed his soft right hand on my forearm.

"Young man, if you can keep your horses happy and your wagon running straight, and can keep up with the rest of us, you'll come out of this trip a man. And something else, like I told some of the others, how about dispensing with naming me chief all the time? From now on, just call me Talking Rock."

"Yes sir, Talking Rock! " I said as I gave him a hearty handshake, man to man. A new confidence took hold of me. Ma joined me along with the Roartys.

So that was how it came about with me taking over wagon 3.

I recall the time earlier in East Tenn-a'see when Talking Rock brought our wagon train to a stop and told us drivers that we would be fording the French Broad River. It looked fearsome, being wide and lively. "You drivers will need to put someone on your brake handles so you can get your wagons down the bank and into the water without difficulty."

It tickled me good when Ma walked up to the front bench and grabbed hold of the brake lever, helping us to ease into the river as smooth as silk. We quickly ran into a swift current, though. Water swirled halfway up on our wheels. That didn't bother me much because the first two wagons had made it all right and my four horses danced easily across the rocky river bed. Then out there in the middle of the river, I decided the horses needed a little break, so I halted the team in midstream so they could slurp up their bait of water.

Ma kept a daily journal on our trip. She showed me several, one of which went like this:

*Spent the night without incident near Newport, Tenn-a'see. We are now in the hands of God and our kind guides from the Cherokee Nation, Chief Talking Rock and his wonderful wife Gilda Golden-feather. We feel confident that they will lead us safely to our new home in the Hi-wass'ee Valley, where we can help spread the word of our Lord amongst the Cherokee people.*

*We continue to grieve about the sad passing of my beloved husband, whose memory continues to burn brightly in our hearts and minds. We pray for God's continued guidance . . .*

One of the things Talking Rock did on the trip that endeared him to us all was taking time to give us little history lessons during breaks or on overnight stops. I remember him telling us when we stopped in the old Cherokee Overhill country that, "Just over a half century ago, this area was a bloody killing field between white settlers and angry Cherokee guerillas."

Everybody wanted more details, so the chief took time for a little lecture.

"For thousands of years," I recalled his saying, "the Cherokees occupied all of what is today Tenn-a'see and Kentuck, plus the western ends of North and South Carolina plus big chunks of Virginia, north Georgee and northeast Al'a-bam'a.

"But a sad tragedy came in the mid 1700s," he said, "when the Cherokees' great Beloved Man, Att'a-kul'la-kul'la, and his old chiefs such as O-con'os'to'ta pretty much gave away to white speculators millions of acres of Cherokee land up in here and Kentuck for a few wagon loads of baubles and trinkets."

The chief went on to tell us that the Beloved Man's son, Draggin' Canoe, the pockmark faced warrior, a victim of the earlier smallpox epidemic, exploded in anger and stomped out of the signing ceremony.

"That was on March 14, 1775," Talking Rock said. "Just before the start of the Revolutionary War. In the months to follow, Draggin' Canoe led a thousand Cherokees from their East Tenn-a'see settlements and resettled them a hundred miles to the southwest. There they were joined by a thousand angry Creek Indians who had lost their own homes to white settlers in southwest Georgia."

"Where exactly did they all end up?" I asked.

"High up on the back side of Lookout Mountain, Jon, past the Moccasin Bend of the great Tenn-a'see River; it was his sanctuary for carrying out an unending series of scalping and killing forays against the white intruders and also supporting the British cause against the rebel American whites. Draggin' Canoe's warriors called themselves Chickamaugans for a river by that name. And for decades, backed by British and Creek allies, they waged a bloody war against the white settlements up and down the Holston, the Little Tenn-a'see and the Hi-wass'ee Rivers. And in Kentuck and middle Tenn-a'see, that for hundreds of years had been the Cherokees' vast hunting grounds.

"Naturally," Talking Rock added, "the white pioneers fought back furiously, led by Nol-li'chuck'ee Jack Sevier, who became Tenn-a'see's first governor. So we had a bloody war that went on for years and years. The reason was that the British down in Pensacola, Florida, were providing Draggin' Canoe's rebels with rifles, bullets and black powder. They called it *ball and powder*."

"How in the world did they get all those munitions up to Draggin' Canoe's hilltop hideaway?" I asked.

"On the backs of mules," he replied. "Hundreds of mules. Every week or so, a long line of pack mules trudged up from Pensacola and wound their way up to Draggin' Canoe's stronghold, loaded down with the war munitions."

"Unbelievable," wheelwright Goliath Dan said. "And how did peace ever come about?"

"One night Draggin' Canoe's British allies suddenly pulled out of Florida, abandoning their Pensacola warehouse."

"So, without ammunition, I guess that put a stop to the bloody raids," declared Conrad Carreker, our blacksmith.

"It sure did," Talking Rock replied. "As the word got out, agents from Tenn-a'see swarmed in to buy up much of the remaining Cherokee lands. And with the end of the Revolutionary War a few years later, peace finally reached the tattered Cherokee Nation. By then the nation's boundaries had shrunk by more than two thirds."

It saddened me just thinking about what had happened to the poor Cherokees after their great and generous leader Att'a-kul'la-kul'la ("the Little Carpenter") had sold them out to the Carolina land speculators. Of course, I heard later that the revered chief was under severe pressure first from the British and then from the Americans, who were about to win the Revolutionary War.

Eventually, the chief told us, when the Americans ran the British out of North America, the Scotch-Irish sharp-shooters, returning home in victory including the one at King's Mountain, took even more retribution against the poor Cherokee villages in East Tenn-a'see.

Now it became clear to me why the Little Carpenter had no other choice but to surrender. A sad ending to the life of the great Chief Att'a-kul'la-kul'la.

# CHAPTER NINE

## A Special Welcome & Angry Priests

Indians were swarming into our community from every which way. "Looks like the start up of a Methodist camp meeting," Ma said when we walked outdoors. "Wonder what might be the occasion?"

"Don't you know?" Preacher Paul asked as he walked past. "They're coming to celebrate your arrival, all you newcomers. We tried to keep it a secret but we imagined you'd hear about it, particularly when Talking Rock had our students out digging the barbecue pits yesterday."

I noticed plumes of smoke rising from the hollow. The breeze wafting our way smelled so savory I decided to go down to see what was cooking. I found Gilda Goldenfeather and Naomi, the mission cook, supervising a half dozen scholars who had been working in shifts through the night, I learned, tending pits of hot coals cooking up a big barbecue. It was an amazing sight: pork and venison hams and shoulders were sizzling away over a grill of green hickory saplings.

Over on the side, Jacob, Naomi's husband, was stirring a big cast iron pot of what he called Brunswick Stew. "We're using squirrels as the primary meat," he said. "That'll give the stew a special taste."

Meanwhile, the lines of Cherokees coming our way swelled. Trails were clogged. Most were of the visitors were walking in family groups, but some were riding horses and I saw some families riding two-wheel steer wagons, a popular local contraption pulled by a single steer or horse.

"How did they get the word?" I asked Corn Silk.

"Preacher Paul sent runners yesterday to all the villages inviting them to attend the celebration," he replied. "Many left home at the crack of dawn."

"Where are they going to be lodged tonight?" Ma asked.

"Lodged?" the linkster laughed. "They'll lodge themselves, Mistress Rebecca; most will camp out in the open. They're well used to accommodating themselves whatever the circumstance."

Late in the afternoon, the visitors lined up at the barbecue pits and received their portions in cane baskets and the stew in clay bowls. "This looks like an old timey dinner-on-the-grounds like those we used to have at our church in Virginia," I told Wa-gu'li, who had walked up with his mother Su-ta'li.

Near sundown, everyone found places to sit in the meadow fronting the mission church. Oak Tree and Goliath Dan circled the grounds, lighting the torches, and Hawkeye Hawkins brought out the church's well worn lectern, a four foot hollowed out gum log that was set straight up with a flat pine board nailed down across the top.

The student choir gathered in front and started singing some old hymns in the darkening twilight. One was a favorite of mine from childhood and Ma and I sang along, using our familiar words:

> *Love divine, all loves excelling,*
> *Joy of heaven to earth come down.*
> *Fix in us thy humble dwelling,*
> *All thy faithful mercies crown.*

Preacher Paul welcomed everyone and said the church was pleased to celebrate the arrival of "our wonderful new missionaries." Then he introduced Merlin as the featured speaker. The newcomer from Charleston proceeded to give something of a short sermon telling about God's love and redemption, and calling on everyone to pray hard, confess their sins and ask for God's grace and forgiveness. In turn, he said, God would give them life eternal.

The next day as the visitors departed our grounds, I heard talk about the presence of angry *Ad-hon'ski* priests during the event the night before. Conrad Carreker said he "saw several of them sitting atop their horses out on the fringe of the crowd."

I went next door to Talking Rock's place to find out more. Goliath Dan and Kindness were there. The chief confirmed that several conjurers had indeed galloped up on their fine horses about the time the singing got under way. "They didn't join the crowd," he said. "Instead, they hung back and stayed in their saddles, just beyond the light of the torches, watching and listening."

"I saw them, too," Goliath Dan said. "There were eight or ten of them. And I heard talk that the priests had become angry with Preacher Paul and also the Methodist circuit riders who've been preaching against the Indians' old ways—late night dancing, ball plays, gambling, and the people's right to practice polygamy."

"Polygamy?" Kindness Haughton asked.

"Yes indeed," Talking Rock said. "It's pretty common among some of the head men and wealthier Cherokees. A number of them have two or three wives."

"Do tell! " Kindness implored.

Talking Rock confirmed that conjurer anger was indeed on the rise. "They're losing control of their people," he said, "and they're blaming us." He went on to explain the problem:

"You have to realize that Persimmon Creek and the Hi'wass'ee River have been sacred to the older Cherokees and their conjurer priests around here from time immemorial," he said. "Those waterways have several places where the priests perform their rituals and the natives go to the water to get their past sins wiped out. And on special occasions such as the ball play, that's where the athletes go before each game for an *Ad-hon'ski* blessing, including being scratched on their backs with bear claws."

"And I've seen full-blood men going early of a morning to the water for their holy immersions," Goliath Dan declared, "looking toward the rising sun and praying to their Great Spirit. Recently, I saw an entire Cherokee family visiting a river spot to go through the Cherokee water rituals."

"Absolutely true," Talking Rock said. "Unfortunately, the Cherokees' absolution pool there in Persimmon Creek is exactly where we baptize our new converts. It's becoming popular with younger Cherokees who join our church. Tomorrow morning, for instance, Preacher Paul plans a baptismal ceremony right there in the pool that the priests have used over the years for their absolution rituals."

The chief added that the mission church's Cherokee converts are told that when they are baptized and become Christians, they are cleansed permanently and that their past sins will be forgiven forever. "In other words," he said, "they don't need to go to the water every so often in the old Cherokee way. That fact is taking hold of many of the young mixed-breed Indians."

"No wonder the priests are angry," Kindness said. "They're not only losing control of their river, they are fast losing the allegiance of their people."

"I'm afraid it's all too true," Talking Rock said. "And it could become something of a problem for our entire mission family."

Later that night, we all gathered at Merlin's cabin and told him what we were hearing.

"Yes," he said. "I understand the chiefs are organizing to reassert their power and Preacher Paul needs to do something to soothe their anger. I'm sure he wouldn't want a civil war breaking out around here with the Cherokees and their shamen."

That night, when I told Ma all about the talk, she had a hard time going to sleep. The more she tried to doze off, the more awake she became.

"Don't let your heart be troubled, Ma," I said, quoting one of my favorite Bible verses. "We're surrounded by many friends here: Merlin, Talking Rock and Gilda, Goliath Dan and Kindness, the Carrekers, Hawkeye Hawkins, the Roartys and many sweet Cherokees like Su-ta'li, Corn Silk and Wa-gu'li and of course Oak Tree and Laugh-in'gal."

"You're right, son. But when I married your father, I pledged to stick with him through thick or thin and now that he's gone to be with the Lord, I feel bound to continue working to carry out the mission here. He wouldn't want me to give up. So I'll pray to see if I can find myself more useful around here so we can bring about some sort of reconciliation with our Indian neighbors."

She finally dozed off to sleep. But the conversation left me thinking into the night. I decided that I would have to go to my knees in prayer a lot more often, to help Ma get her confidence back and also to ask God how we can win back the love and respect of the Cherokees in our midst, including the full-blood *Ad-hon'ski* priests who seem bent on starting a war against our missionaries.

# CHAPTER TEN

## Ma Takes to the Cherokees

The warm breezes of springtime sweeping down the valley helped Ma to decide to stop worrying about the full-blood priests and instead throw her energy into helping the ordinary Cherokee people. With the green buds of early May beginning to swell, she called her science classroom to attention. "Children," she announced, "I have a surprise for you today. After our opening prayer, we'll spend the day outdoors."

Loud handclaps followed. It was hard to see who was more excited, the children or Ma. She had already picked out the place—a spot the Cherokees call *Tak-a'tuka*—the Double Springs. Soon we were on our way, skipping in the springtime sun.

"Miz Merion," Gu'li asked as we walked, "can we take off our shoes and moccasins today? Can we?" His question soon swelled into a chorus. "We'll see," Ma replied. The sun was sending down warm rays onto the pungent woods earth and the warm winds had a soothing gentleness that told us the time of Earth's annual rebirth was at hand.

When we reached the Double Springs, I could see why Ma loved the place so much. The springs straddled a beautiful beech tree and the water from each side came together as one in creating the branch below.

"Children, you know we've been studying about nature. I want each of you to go out and bring back a plant or a twig or a leaf and identify it for me. If you give me a correct answer, you can pull off your footwear."

Well sir, it looked like a bunch of race horses at the starting gate, the way the kids shot out into the woods, including Wa-gu'li and me.

The first scholar to return was Little Deer, who ran up to Ma with a red root.

"This is bloodroot, Miz Merion. Under the white flower and green leaves is the root. We have used this root as a medicine for years and also to paint our faces and bodies red."

"Excellent, Little Deer! Go ahead and pull off your moccasins," Ma said.

Gu'li got to remove his shoes when he walked back with a plant he identified as ramps. "Don't you chew on this root raw, Miz Merion. It will give you a horrible stink for weeks, a horrible stink! "

Our little excursion turned out to be a big celebration that day in the woods as my classmates and I brought in trilliums, silver bells, ginseng, white violets, daffodils, black locust and others. Soon the students were jumping up and down in bare feet and Ma let us roam for a while about the meadow that had been blanketed with wild strawberries earlier in the year.

Going barefooted obviously came naturally to the Cherokee youth, as I guess it does to children all over the world in springtime's first warm days. I remembered shedding my shoes around May first up in Virginia. I relished the times I could follow in the path of my Pa as he used a horse to plow our garden patch. The soft, warm earth gave my toes a delightful tingle, putting new life into my springtime step.

Ma used the barefoot experience to teach her lesson that day. She called us to attention as we returned to the classroom.

"Children, just over a month ago, March twenty-first, marked the vernal equinox. That's the first day of spring, the time of year when the length of day and of night are equal. From then on, the amount of daylight grows every day until the peak of late summertime arrives and when corn nears maturity. Trees are now leafing out and will soon provide shade for all of us in the hot summer.

"All of this order is a magnificent gift from God," she added, "a God who created our universe and whose son came to Earth eighteen hundred years ago in the form of a human being. Do you know his name?"

"Jesus! " they shouted almost in unison.

The students had questions, though. Walking Tall asked, "Miz Merion, did Jesus have hands and feet and eyes and ears like us? And did he enjoy going barefoot?"

"Oh yes, Walking Tall. He had eyes and ears, hands and feet just like you. And I'm sure that when he was a young boy growing up in the Galilee region near the Jordan River north of Jerusalem, he loved pulling off his sandals in their springtime and would briefly walk barefoot in the sandy desert. But not in the hot summer months that were to come. He had sandals for that."

Another scholar spoke up, a shy girl LuAnne, named for a widow's mite lady in Charleston.

"Did Jesus look like us?" she asked. "Did he have a brown skin like ours, or was he a white man with a splotchy face like the Georgians?"

"Where did you get to know Georgians, LuAnne?"

"We lived down at Ku-sa'watt-ee," she said, "and we saw many Una'ka Georgians and palefaces from Virginia and Carolina, passing by on the Federal Road, going to Nash- ville and into Al-a'bam'a."

"To answer your question, LuAnne, most likely Jesus had a skin similar to your Cherokee skin. Where he grew up in the Middle East, there was lots of sunshine and over the years the people there developed a darker, thicker skin, the better to withstand the harsh rays of the sun."

LuAnne persisted. "Miz Merion, some of the whites who traveled through Ku-sa'watt'ee said we Indians were worthless. They muttered something like, 'Damn savages, they're no better than the nigger slaves they have amongst 'em.'"

Ma turned angry. She stood up and raised her voice, one of the few times I can recall. "Listen, children. Just remember that whoever utters something like that is rude and it is they who are the savages. LuAnne, I would imagine that only a few of them can read and write like you can. So just overlook them. The Bible teaches us not to judge people, but the important thing for you to remember is this: You children have been made in God's image, just as Jesus was. You are precious in His sight. You are beautiful. Every one of you is beautiful. And you are intelligent. I am proud of you. So just ignore those uncouth Georgians."

I sure was proud of Ma that day and Gu'li told me he was, too.

Warmer weather was coming on, and I was happy when school turned out for the summer. Ma liked that, too, and one bright day she mounted her favorite mission horse, Sa-da'yi, and started taking short trips every day to the homes of Cherokees and whites up and down the valley— those who attended the mission church services and those she hoped would start.

Everywhere she went, she had words of encouragement in the art of everyday living, particularly housekeeping. "Cleanliness is next to godliness," she would say.

Using corn shucks and homemade lye soap to clean tables and floors (for those who had wooden floors), she urged housewives to keep their places sparkling clean.

She also challenged them to take time to enjoy the flowering plants blooming everywhere, particularly the rhododendrons and wild azaleas. But one day she found herself learning a lesson from an Indian, with one of her students serving as her linkster.

"Mister Tu-lus'kee," she asked, "Is that a sourwood tree you are cutting down?"

"Yes, Mission Lady. We need wood for fireplace, to cook with."

"What about the bees? Don't they love the nectar from the sourwoods?"

"Yes, Mission Lady. Bees make sweet honey from sourwood blossoms."

"Wouldn't it be good to bypass the sourwood and cut an oak for firewood?"

"Not good to take down oak, Mission Lady."

"Why not?"

"Bears depend on acorns as their food."

"Oh, I see. I suppose you feel the same about the chestnut and hickory trees?"

"Yes, ma'am. And chinquapins."

"Pardon me for intruding on your world, Mister Tu-lus'kee. I'm sure you'll do whatever you think best."

Tu'-lus'kee then told the linkster that perhaps he could possibly reconsider and cut down a few poplar trees for firewood instead of sourwoods, even though the poplar tulip blossoms gave squirrels delicious meals throughout the springtime.

"Folks in the valley are beginning to look forward to your mother's visits," Talking Rock told me.

I took my pony, Bullet, and joined Ma on one of her trips. I was amazed at the response. "It's the mission lady!" the kids would yell when they spotted her horse, running back to tell their mothers. In time, Cherokee women and men, as well as the white settler families, began to see many new possibilities in life, thanks to the "mission lady."

With Ma's encouragement, the transplanting of flaming azaleas around their cabins became a popular pastime. "Gorgeous, Su-ta'li, just gorgeous," Ma said one day as she admired a clump of native azaleas that Corn Silk dug up in the woods and set out next to her cabin door. I could see from Su-ta'li's smile that she loved the compliment.

Ma's suggestions naturally were made in a loving spirit. Corn Silk told me that when Ma was around the Indians they never felt they were being looked down upon.

One day out of the blue, Rachel Fishing Hawk, the wife of a Cherokee exhorter, told Preacher Paul, "The mission lady, she is a saint."

Even Missionary Merlin began to appreciate the higher possibilities of the human soul when Ma brought new insights to his attention. Thanks to her, Merlin, Gu'li and I came to appreciate sunsets and sunrises as godly works of art. The setting of the sun became a great attraction. Ma often spent a quarter hour just watching as the sun settled in the west and as the clouds on the horizon shifted as if being painted on God's palette.

"Your mother seems to be in a trance as the sun goes down," Merlin said. "And, thanks to her, I have begun to enjoy the evening skies. Last night, I was amazed when streaks of Indian yellow spread across the western horizon as the sun faded gently into the evening darkness." Only after such a long watch would Ma regain her consciousness and smile as if she'd been in touch with the Almighty himself. "God must have had fun making the world," she would say at odd moments, reminding Gu'li and me of the talks we have about the mysteries of the universe.

Like I said earlier, Ma showered love and affection on Cherokees of all walks of life, low and high. But one of her most difficult ordeals occurred just a few months after we arrived, when she had to expel a twelve-year-old half-breed who had disrupted classes with her haughtiness. The girl, who was intelligent and could speak English well, carried the name of her benefactor in Boston, Marguerite Jones.

Faithfully every month a small contribution came in the mail from Matron Jones with a letter inquiring about the little Indian girl carrying her name. After several difficulties with the girl, Ma responded to Mrs. Jones that, "regretfully, Marguerite has acted arrogant and ungrateful and therefore her identity has been transferred to another child, a full-blood who, while not quite as advanced in speaking English, nevertheless has a pure heart and an open mind to learning."

Within a year after we arrived, Cherokees in the valley adopted Ma as an honorary Cherokee. *Ta-wa'di*, the Hawk, one of the nation's head men, bestowed on her the name, *Tu'ti'yi*, the Cherokee word for Snowbird, and called her, "The Snowbird Lady." Ma loved it and began signing her correspondence "Tu-ti'yi, nee Rebecca Merion."

# CHAPTER ELEVEN

## Spying on Ephraim Coward

By the time the summer arrived, Wa-gu'li and I had been on several spying trips up and down the valley and managed to get back home free and clear every time.

"The reason for our good fortune," I told Gu'li, "is because angels have been looking after us. Our God keeps a bunch of 'em flying around in the sky day and night," I said. "They're on call to help folks who have the belief." I knew Gu'li didn't put much store in such things, but he admitted something was giving us powerful protection during our roving about.

Then one day when we were walking back from our Secret Place, Gu'li took me by surprise with a plan for another spying mission. "I heard that Eph Coward is getting ready to run off a batch of recipe at his still down in the Wa'la-si'li cove," he said. "Let's go spy on him."

I looked at Gu'li a minute or two and took off my coonskin cap, scratched my head, and studied on it. "Sounds awful risky," I said. "If Preacher Paul should find out about it, he'd church me out of the mission, and most likely would send me packing my bags back to Virginia."

"Anything like this always carries a little risk," he said. "Let's be courageous."

"If you're so set on it, Gu'li," I said, "count me in."

We decided to start out first by fishing a little the next day, which was a Saturday. Our folks saw the logic in that, and Ma gave me permission to go, so I got out of bed before sunup—that's Talking Rock's normal "getting-up time"— and I walked next door to his cabin. Gilda Golden-feather met me at the door. She had a coffee pot steaming away in the fireplace.

"Morning, T'san," she said. "What brings you here so early?"

"Gu'li and I are planning to go fishing," I said. "And I didn't want to wake Ma. She knows all about it." (Of course I realized that while I told the truth to Ma, I left out the whole truth and that caused me to worry some about it in my own mind.)

"Well, you need something to get you started out right," Gilda said. "Let me give you a cup of coffee." Apparently Talking Rock had already eaten and left home.

She also brought out a serving of hot biscuits from her spider skillet, the kind of biscuits that made for a wonderful coffee soakee. "This is just great for a starter," I told Gilda. "We'll be frying us some fish later on when we get down to the creek. That should keep us going for the rest of the day."

That coffee soakee really hit the spot. Even though I have grown up enough to drink coffee straight, I continue to enjoy coffee soakee every chance I get. I've even talked Gu'li into enjoying coffee-soakee of a morning. Only fair since he's got me eating Cherokee *con'a-han'ee*, a corn mush that I never thought I'd ever get used to. Now I relish it almost as much as Ma's hominy grits. Speaking of con'a-han'ee, I've greatly enjoyed visiting Cherokee homes where the mothers keep pots of con'a-han'ee bubbling warm all day and night at their fireplaces. And when a visitor walks in the door, he's obliged to first stop by the con'a-han'ee pot and enjoy a few sups or else he's considered haughty and downright unfriendly. So, every time I go to Gu'li's house, or any other Cherokee cabin as far as that's concerned, I know to first head to the con'a-han'ee pot and get me a gourd full. That proves my neighborliness.

Most Cherokees I know are downright friendly, anyhow, just like most of the valley's palefaces, excepting I guess the Coward moonshining family. 'Course all I know about the Cowards is hear-tell, particularly from Gilda Goldenfeather. She let me know her feelings about them shortly after our arrival in the Cherokee Nation. "Boy you'd better stay away from them scoundrels if you know what's good for you," she said. But I'd learned that Talking Rock was on friendly terms with Eph Coward when it comes to hunting bears and such, so I decided to reserve my judgment about him and his family until I could get a chance to meet and talk to him man to man.

To get back on track of what I was relating, after making sure Su-ta'li would be coming to help Ma, and after getting the coffee soakee from Gilda, Wa-gu'li and I got together and headed south. We first fished Persimmon Creek for a while and ate us a mess of Ku'sa bass. Then we headed toward Eph Coward's place. Lo and behold, no sooner had we reached the U-ni'coi Turnpike than we ran into a big bunch of turkeys. We heard their racket way before we saw them. As they came around the bend, the big toms were chattering away.

We stopped at an oak tree beside the road and watched the parade pass. I'd heard tell of such droving spectacles but it was the first time I'd ever seen one. I was attracted to the big toms in front as they pranced along with their heads swaying proudly like puppets, and showing off their red combs and their shaggy black goatees that hung down almost a foot long.

Then, on the back end of the procession, here came two mixed-breed Indians carrying long hickory sticks, pushing the turkeys on down the road. Gu'li recognized them as trader Murphy's mixed-breed grandsons.

"They're drovers," Gu'li whispered. "They'll run those gobblers all the way to Augusta, and come back with a load of goods for Murphy's trading post—calico cloth for the women, and nails, axes, hoes and such for the men. Plus guns and black powder and barrels of coffee beans and salt."

As soon as the turkeys passed here came a whole bunch of grunting hogs, along with *their* drovers. They weren't so numerous, and sure enough, right behind the last drover came the provision wagon, driven by another one of Murphy's people, a full-blood Cherokee.

"The whole bunch will stop off tonight at somebody's cowpens," Gu'li said. "They'll group the hogs together in a pen and burn fires and post a guard all night to keep out marauding bears, wolves and painters. And, of course, the turkeys will fly up onto tree limbs nearby, out of harm's way."

Well sir, that drover parade was something to see, but it delayed our spying trip for more than a half hour. As soon as the tail-end wagon passed out of sight, we crossed the pike and got back on the trail. By the time we reached Wa-la'si'li Creek, the sun was way up in the sky. We climbed a high-up hill and surveyed the terrain. "We're right near Eph Coward's cabin," Gu'li said. "See that plume of smoke? That's his place."

We slipped down closer for a better look, still keeping our cover in the woods and vines. The place looked right pleasant, cut out of the valley forest near the creek. Only thing I saw out of place was a bunch of dead oaks around the edge of the fields. Tree ghosts, they looked like, with blackened trunks and silver limbs pointing pitiful-like into the sky.

"They've been girdled," Wa-gu'li said. I could see the rings chopped around tree trunks about knee high. "That's how they starve a tree to death," he told me. "Of course, Indians have been known to do a similar thing on a smaller scale over the years, as well as burning off fields in early March to rid them of insects and clearing the ground for spring planting."

Gu'li went on to tell me more. "When people come along with their axes and girdle a poor old tree it just stands there and cries and bleeds and shrivels up and finally starves to death. Eventually all the girdled trees fall to the ground and are burned and the following spring. After the rough work digging or burning the stumps, the new ground becomes a field for growing corn, beans and squash. That's what the Cherokees call the three sisters."

The Coward home was a double-pen cabin built of notched logs, and on one side a wide rock chimney. All around were outhouses built of logs and poles. Gu'li identified one of them as a corncrib, a smoke house where they salt down their pork and deer meat and then hang it up for months of smoking and salting.

"I don't see any sign of life," I said.

"The men folk are likely out at the still," Gu'li said. "And I imagine the women are in the house cooking and maybe spinning and weaving cloth. Dessie Mae Longwillow, Eph's wife, is probably fixing the noontime meal for the crowd at work."

Looking east, we saw another plume of smoke going

straight up in the air. "That's where the still is," Gu'li said. "And that straight up smoke tells us our scent won't be picked up by Eph's dogs." Even so, we circled around to the back-side of their place. It took us a while climbing, but we figured that'd be a lot safer.

"Eph Coward isn't trying to hide anything here," Gu'li said quietly. "The Cherokee head men and conjurer priests know all about his enterprise and are some of his best customers. But he wouldn't put up with us coming in on him without being invited beforehand. In particular since we're part of the missionary crowd."

From our vantage point, our ears picked up a steady racket of "still sounds." We could see and hear the roaring flames whipping around the copper pot and up the back end of the furnace chimney. And we could hear the sound of water pouring, the clanging of buckets and of wood being chopped.

Well sir, when we got where we could see plain, it appeared most of the Coward family, their dogs, mules and all, were all right there at work. "Look, T'san," Gu'li said, "you can see the round copper pot and its furnace cut into a hillside next to that branch of water." Two strapping men were chopping wood off to the side. Another had the job of toting the firewood up to the rock furnace, while still another was using a long-forked stick to stir the soupy stuff in the wooden barrels. "They're mash barrels," Gu'li whispered. "See how each one is lashed together with hickory straps all around? The blackberry pomace probably has been fermenting in those barrels for a few days. That's what causes the sour smells. Eph likely put in a gallon of ground-up sprouted rye malt into each of the barrels to speed up fermentation, along with a lot of sweet sorghum syrup. When the fermenting mash stops bubbling, they'll have what they call blackberry wine. Then they'll distill that wine into the brandy recipe."

"Is that the old man in the middle?" I asked.

"You're right, T'san. That's Eph Coward himself right there where the recipe will soon be pouring out." I noticed a young woman helping out and golly was she good look-ing, with curvy legs and bright red hair falling down her back. She was near what Gu'li said was the condenser bar-rel that they called a flake stand.

"They keep that barrel filled with cool water to condense the alcoholic steam flowing across from the still pot to the curled copper worm in the barrel," he said. "That's where the alcohol is extracted from the water at a temperature of about 176 degrees. Which of course is much lower than the 212 degrees boiling temperature of water."

"Gu'li, how in tarnation do you know so much about an operation such as this?"

"My father, who went by the name Jim Eagle, worked for Eph as a still hand and brought me here with him several times. That was before Pa went off to fight in the Creek War in A'la-bam'a with the Cherokee brigade."

I couldn't keep my eyes off the beautiful red head. Ever

once in a while, she'd go fetch another little barrel for Eph to use to catch the fresh recipe singlings.

"What's that gal's name?" I asked.

"Rosalee. She's Eph's granddaughter. They call her Rose. She's filled out a lot since I saw her last. She's sure not a child anymore."

We hunkered down and watched and listened. The old man was talking:

"Abe," I heard him say, "get Faron to hep you bring up some more of them hickory logs. Make haste. We're about through with these singlins."

Before we arrived, I had pictured Eph Coward to be a tall man, from the way Wa-gu'li had described him. He was stout all right, but he was short and squat, but with a right healthy chest and big muscular arms. And he had a bright red face and a pug nose along with thinning red hair.

I could see that his boys moved fast when the old man spoke. Ever so often I'd see him shaking a little bottle and then looking at the bubbles standing on the surface. "They call that 'reading the bead'," Gu'li said, "checking the proof. After that, Eph usually takes a swig from that tiny bottle."

I thought to myself that Eph's raspy high tenor voice was likely caused by his constant likker drinking on the job and off. Gu'li said drinking like that was harmful to a body and that we should not ever be drinking any of his alcoholic products at any time.

"I'm sorry these people have so many Cherokee customers," I said, "particularly the young men."

"I couldn't agree more," Gu'li said.

We didn't stay long, in light of the fact that Eph Coward had an awful name for fighting, and his boys likewise,
particular when he's full of his own makin's, which I think
was the case today.

We skedaddled out of there pretty quick, retracing our
steps back home. We made good time. Before we reached
Persimmon Creek, though, rain started coming down, first
in the form of sprinkles. Then the skies opened up with
flashes of lightning and thunder raking across the valley.

"Those skies look awful mean for this time of year,"
Gu'li said. Before we'd walked very far going back home,
we got doused good with a heavy downpour. Arriving later
back at the mill house, we found the waters of Persimmon
Creek rising and angry, and way up over its banks.

"We'd be foolish to try to ford the creek with it like this,"
Gu'li said. "That deluge would almost wash us away."

We climbed up onto the overhead foot-bridge. It was
swaying back and forth in the wind, but I prayed an unspoken prayer and put myself into Guli's hands and followed him across, holding tight to the rope-size grape vine
on top that went clear across the stream. Eventually we
reached the beech tree on the other side and climbed down
on the ladder to the bank. Boy was I relieved! We raced
home, soaking wet.

I was convinced God's angels had been watching over

us all the way and I said an unspoken prayer, thanking the Good Lord for keeping us in the palm of his hands throughout the day and what was becoming a stormy night.

Ma was mighty glad to see me when I walked in and I was happy that she didn't rare at me.

# CHAPTER TWELVE

## The Storm

The following day, an awful thunderstorm brought terrible affliction into our valley. On the second night, it turned even worse, including high winds and earthshaking thunder and lightning.

"It's a real gully washer," Hawkeye Hawkins told us when he stopped by our cabin. After getting Ma's permission, I put on my duds, including my raincoat and new deerskin boots, and ran next door to Talking Rock's cabin. Goliath Dan was there.

"We're praying that this thing will end soon," Dan was telling the chief. "You know the mill sits atop those oak stilts. If the dam gives way, the whole mill could very well wash away, too."

After hearing that, I felt more worried than ever, and it didn't help matters when Talking Rock's cabin started shaking from the winds. A knock came at the door.

"Who be ye?" Talking Rock yelled.

"Conrad and Merlin."

"Pull the latch string, fellers," he yelled. They walked in soaking wet. "I believe it's getting worse," Conrad Carreker said as he entered.

"You're right," Goliath Dan replied. "The situation down there at the mill is getting awful precarious. Oak Tree is worried that the dirt dam might give way."

"I've been afraid this very thing could happen," Talking Rock said.

Mister Carreker brought even more bad news. "There's still over two hundred bushels of shelled corn and a lot more ear corn sitting there in the mill house that the scholars brought in from the fields last week."

After praying about it for a while, they agreed, despite the risks involved, to take action to try to save the corn. "Conrad," Talking Rock said, "how about you and Dan get out a steer wagon and a horse and have teacher Roarty pick four of his stoutest scholars and take them down to the mill? Merlin and Jon and I will follow you in a second wagon and we'll congregate at Dan's cabin across from the mill."

After the first wagon left, Merlin and I hitched up another horse and wagon. I raced to our cabin to tell Ma what I was doing. She was sound asleep, so I ran out and jumped in the wagon. The wind was whistling through the trees and the rain was coming down in sheets. Lightning spread across the sky like a spider web, followed by sharp claps of thunder. When the lightning lit up the way, Talking Rock popped the reins and off we went.

"Reminds me of a hurricane we had one time in Charleston," Merlin yelled. I don't think Talking Rock heard him because of the noise. Right about then, lightning struck a tree directly ahead of us, and the glowing current spun around the tree from top to bottom. The crashing thunder caused my ears to pop. The horse reared and pawed the air like she was trying to climb the tree. The wagon flipped, slinging out Merlin and me. Another fork of lightning lit up the sky, skipping across the tree tops. I was mighty happy when I saw Talking Rock getting up without serious injury.

"You hurt, boy?" he asked me.

"I'm all right, but I'm afraid Merlin got hit when he fell out."

When another lightning strike lit up the skies, we could see Merlin lying there like a dish rag with his eyes closed and a black mark on his forehead.

"*Merlin wake up!*" Talking Rock yelled, kneeling down beside him. "You can't die on us, son," he added. "You just got here; wake up!"

Then he pulled out a little flask of root bitters from his coat pocket and poured a few drops on Merlin's lips. The missionary's eyes flickered open and he asked what was happening.

"This here thunderstorm is what's happening, Merlin!"

"Oh, yes, now I remember."

"Here, take a swaller of this."

"What is it?"

"Cherokee bitters. It's good for what ails you."

The missionary sipped a swallow and made a terrible face.

"That's awful!" he said, pushing the bottle away.

Talking Rock and I managed to lift Merlin into the wagon and we took him back to Preacher Paul's house and asked him to care for the young missionary. Then we headed down to the mill. When we arrived, Goliath Dan had some good news. "The rain is slacking off a little," he said, "and praise the Lord, the mill house appears to be holding up all right for the time being. I'm still worried about the dam, though. Let's go over and you can see the situation for yourself." Dan told the students and others to wait in Dan's house.

I followed along as Dan led Talking Rock across the road to the mill house, using light from the continuous lightning. I wondered if they'd lost their senses, going back out to the mill house with the dam situation being so fragile. Once we got inside the frame building, we could hear the water wheel whirling madly. We waited for the next flash of lightning so we could see. Well sir, then a double flash of lightning crossed the sky and just about blinded us. Smoke started pouring from the mill house roof, but the rains squelched the flames in short order and I figured we were rescued again by God's angels.

It was a depressing sight. After taking a look at the stored corn, we rushed back out, moving ahead every time we got some light from the stormy skies. Talking Rock got everyone's attention in Dan's cabin and spoke a little prayer for help from the Good Lord. Meanwhile, Laugh-in'gal, Oak Tree's wife, came over from next door with a big pot of con'a-han'ee. Everyone joined in, getting their share.

While we were eating, the house shook with a windy blast, then suddenly, there came a strange silence.

"Do y'all hear what I'm not hearing?" Talking Rock said.

"Like what?" Hawkeye asked, putting down his gourd of con'a-han'ee.

"It's turned quiet out there," the chief said. "And I believe the rain and the wind have stopped."

Hawkeye swung open Dan's front door and, sure enough, the wind had calmed down, and the early morning skies were clearing. All was quiet except the drip-drip-drip of raindrops clearing off the shingled roof.

"Well I'll be dog," Goliath Dan said.

"Hurry and finish eating, fellers," Talking Rock shouted. "We need to get to work. It's getting light out. The clouds have blown away."

Then Talking Rock and Conrad Carreker led the way as all of us, including the scholars, joined in moving baskets of corn from inside the mill up to the front door. The students then took two steers and sledded the corn out of harm's way, up to a corncrib.

All of us stretched out in front of Dan's fireplace to dry off and rest. But Oak Tree kept a vigil near the mill house. Two hours later, he came back with some good news.

"Water go down! " he said as he walked in.

"Praise the Lord," Goliath Dan shouted, "I guess the dam's helt."

And so it had. The rain, lightning and thunder had disappeared and the waters of Persimmon Creek got quieter. Goliath Dan and Oak Tree led Talking Rock and the rest of us to the top of the dam. From there we saw the huge hole in the earth dam.

"We've just escaped a monumental disaster," Dan said.

"We sure have," Talking Rock said. "Another hour of that storming rain and the the dam would have given way and the mill house would have washed away."

"We need to thank the good Lord in heaven," Goliath Dan said. "It was a benevolent God who brought about the miracle, an answer to our prayers."

That's what I believed, too, 'cause I had said a few unspoken prayers myself during the stormy night and I felt sure that God was picking up our messages loud and clear. But during the worst of the thunder, lightning and rain, when the storm waters were gushing over the dam, Oak Tree said a tall Indian with copper armbands and wearing only a loin cloth appeared out of nowhere and walked clear across the dam.

"Water shed from him like a turtle," Oak said, his words being linked by Talking Rock.

"Who was it?" Hawkeye asked.

"The Priest of Fire," Oak Tree replied.

The way Talking Rock linked it, repeating Oak Tree's story, during the height of the storm, the priest held his hands in the air and looked heavenward, following which the rain stopped for a few moments and the winds died down. Then, according to Oak Tree's story, the Priest of Fire, *A-sa'la Car-tee-kee*, walked across to the other end of the dam and started chanting, with his arms outstretched, pleading with the Great Spirit to halt the storm.

"That when rain stop," Oak Tree said, being linkstered by Talking Rock. We all just stood and looked on in awe.

From the lively way Oak Tree and Laugh-in'gal talked about it afterward, I knew that the word would soon spread to the whole Cherokee settlement. The Indians' Great Spirit—their Yowah God—had brought about the miracle, they would say, thanks to A-sa'la, the Priest of Fire.

For my part, I whispered an unspoken prayer of thanks again that after four days and nights, the awful storm had come to an end. The sun came out clear and bright and I knew more certain than ever that there surely was a Creator God up there looking over us, He and his angels. And I couldn't wait to tell Ma and Gu'li all about it. But first I needed to go and check up on Merlin and Ma.

# CHAPTER THIRTEEN

## The Panther Attack

It was just before Christmas week and as I opened Gu'li's door, I could smell the supper being cooked by his mother Su-ta'li in her fireplace. It was full of crane pots, spiders, fry pans and Dutch ovens. The meal started off with potatoes  and eggs plus corn bread and sweet milk and ended up with my favorite desert, persimmon pudding. She offered us seconds on the dessert and I took her up on her offer for another helping of that wonderful dish.

As soon as we finished eating supper, Gu'li fixed us pallets near the fireplace so we could go straight to bed. We dropped off to sleep almost immediately, since we were tired from traipsing over the neighborhood all day.

Deep into the night, way past midnight, I jumped up

when Su-ta'li started screaming from her bed on the op-
posite wall.

"*Little Fox! Jon-Boy! Something's clawing on the roof!*"

I slapped the sleep cobwebs from my head and jumped
up. So did Gu'li.

"I hear the scratching too, ma'am," I said. "It sounds like
it's on top of the roof near the chimney. Don't fear Su-ta'li,
I'll go up in the loft and see if I can run it off, whatever it
is."

I was trying awfully hard to act calm and grown up, but
to tell the honest truth, my hair felt like it was standing
straight up like a dog in a fight and I was trying hard to
act more courageous than I really was. I could tell from the
scratching and growling that it was likely a panther, and it
sounded like he was about to break in.

"Gu'li," I screamed. "Get a big fire going; I think we may
have a long tail on the roof!"

I heard more scratching and I thought, "What will I do
if he tries to break in?" I came across a heavy churn stick
and tossed it up into the loft. Then I turned around and
pulled down the old muzzle loader hanging on the wall. I'd
never fired one but I'd watched Pa enough, up in Virginia.
I figured this was the one Gu'li's pa used at Horseshoe
Bend.

My hands were wobbly but I pulled the powder horn and
bag from the wall peg and poured some powder into the
barrel, poked in a patch and some lead shot and rammed
everything in with the rod.

I climbed the ladder up into the loft and got Gu'li to

hand the rifle up to me. It was close quarters up there and I could hear the varmint scratching away. I crawled over near the chimney, dragging the rifle and churn stick behind me. I could see it was going to be difficult getting that long flintlock pointed in the right direction.

Just as I reached the chimney, I smelled a dreadful odor. It sickened me to my stomach. *I knew for certain it was a big cat!!* And I could tell he was real close, with only a few inches separating us. Along with his scratching, he growled with a terrible deep-throated growl, followed by a scream, the same scary panther scream we heard that night up in Tenn-a'see. Just God awful! Forgive my cursing, Lord.

I wanted to turn around and go back down the ladder.

"*It's a long tail for sure, Gu'li!* " I yelled. "*I can smell him; he's right over me! Thank the Lord y'all have a laid-on roof, with logs holding down the oak shingles!*"

I tried to pull the rifle to me with my left hand but the barrel got stuck in the rafters. I took the churn stick with my right hand and beat on the heavy hickory shingles. The scratching stopped. I peeked through a tiny crack between two of the boards. The moonlight gave me a partial view. I couldn't see much but I could hear the animal walking around in a circle. Then I got a quick glimpse.

"*Dear God, Gu'li,*" I yelled. "*He's a big one, twice as long as Talking Rock's hound dog!*"

The creature squalled and started scratching again. I could hear the shingles giving way. I near-bout froze in fear but I slapped the churn stick up against the piece of his paw that was sticking through, and he yelped and ran away.

I knew he would be coming back and I knew it was time for a full-scale spoken prayer. I closed my eyes: "*Dear Lord in heaven,*" I said. "*If it be your will, please keep that long tail from getting in and eating us all alive. Amen.*"

The long muzzle-loader was crossed up catiwampus and I couldn't seem to get it pulled around so I could point it up direct at the roof. Why couldn't I have a shorter rifle? Or a horse pistol? Then I saw it—one of his paws was ripping through. Lord what claws! I took the churn stick again and slapped his paw real hard! He hollered in pain and pulled back! Finally I laid down on my back so I could pull the rifle over on my belly.

At long last, I got the rifle pointed up toward the cat and got my finger on the trigger. Suddenly, the roar of a gunshot rang out. I heard a whining cry. Then everything turned quiet. I collapsed and lay there in silence for a little bit. Apparently the mountain lion had left and I thanked the Lord for answering my pitiful prayer. I took in a long breath, full of relief. But I wondered, "Where did the gun shot come from?"

There was a "hal-oooooo" at the door. I crawled over to the ladder hole. It was Talking Rock followed by Gilda, who ran over and hugged Su-ta'li and asked her how she was doing.

"Scared to death," Su-ta'li said, still shaking a bit, "but

otherwise fine. I'm thankful Little Fox stayed down here with me throughout the big scare, while John Boy was up in the loft."

Talking Rock looked up at me sitting up there at the top of the loft hole, holding the long muzzle loader. "You all right, boy?"

"Yes sir," I replied. "But for a while, I feared that cat was gonna break in on me. I finally got the rifle ready to shoot when I heard a shot outside. That must have scared him off."

"That was me doing the shooting, T'san." Talking Rock said.

"Really? Then thanks a whole bunch, Chief. You just saved my life and that of Gu'li and his mother as well."

Su-ta'li stopped rocking, wiped the tears from her eyes with her apron and then started rocking again.

Just as I was getting ready to come down the ladder, I saw Goliath Dan and Comfort coming in. They had heard the gunshot.

"Hey, boy," Dan said, looking up at me. "What's going on up there?"

"That long tail came close to breaking in the roof," I said. "I was up here right under him and scared to death! "

I hopped off the bottom rung of the ladder, still wobbly on my feet, and everybody greeted me warmly.

"Talking Rock's rifle blast saved us for sure," I said.

"Why didn't you shoot him first?" Talking Rock asked.

"I had my finger on the trigger but you beat me to it."

"Wa-gu'li," he asked, "what were you doing all that

time?"

"I was T'san's backup down here and stood guard over Mother. We got down on our knees and prayed long and hard that T'san would shoot that painter dead."

Talking Rock took over the account from there:

"Just then, I was walking down the hill and I could see the painter in the moonlight, walking around on your roof, Su-ta'li. He was a big one, a huge catamount for sure. Never seen any of 'em get this bold, though, not around here. He must'a been awful hungry."

"*Well, did you kill him?*" Goliath Dan asked.

"No, but I shot off his tail."

"*You did what?*" I asked.

"Yep, there's a long tail laying up there on the roof somewhere."

I walked across the room and hung up the muzzle loader on the wall rack. Kindness must have noticed that I still had the shakes. "You were awfully courageous, T'san," she said, patting my arm. "We're so happy that you came out unhurt."

"Thank you, ma'am," I said, trying to find somewhere to sit down.

Talking Rock, looking around at the circle of folks, told everyone how the evening began. "At twilight," he said, "I had the strangest feeling. The dogs were making an awful racket out in the hog pen and I figured it was a bear or a coon. I got my rifle and climbed to the roof of the corn crib, aiming to shoot whatever it was. A half moon was rising and I could see pretty good. But I must've dozed off.

Next thing I knew, Goodness and Mercy were barking up a storm again. When I looked up I saw there was two of them—big Long Tails—and the first one was carrying off Mercy."

"Mercy?" I asked, worried. "*Is Mercy dead?*"

"'Fraid so, son," Talking Rock said. "It's a powerful loss; Gilda is all tore up."

I couldn't help it but I broke down myself and bawled for a few minutes, remembering the sweet little Cherokee cur.

"I can understand your feelings, Jon. I'm gon'a miss that rascal, too. He and Goodness were awful courageous to stand up to the painters. It was hard to see exactly what happened because the moon went behind a cloud about then, but it looked to me like the cat killed Mercy with a bite to the throat. Then he picked her up in his mouth and loped off with her. Then I walked over and saw the other long tail on your roof, Su-ta'li."

Merlin and Hawkeye walked in.

"You fellers missed all the excitement! " Talking Rock grinned.

"Missed what?" Merlin asked.

"Mountain lion attack. Two big yeller painters. The first 'un took off my dog Mercy, bless her heart, and the second came here and tried to break into Su-ta'li's roof."

"My Lord in heaven! " Merlin said, sounding almost like

he was preaching. But he quickly calmed down and said, quietly, "Thank the Lord they didn't harm any of you."

There was a "*si–looooo*" (hello) at the door. It was Oak Tree, carrying his squirrel rifle on his arm. Talking Rock let him in and repeated the news to him in Cherokee. I could tell that with every telling, the long tails got bigger and meaner.

"Painter give you scare-shakes, T'san-us'di?" Oak Tree laughed, his eyes crinkling with merriment.

"Don't make fun of of Jon-boy," Su-ta'li chided him. "He was getting ready to shoot that big cat with our old muzzle loader. He was acting much like a man. I'm real proud of him."

Talking Rock and Oak Tree resumed talking in Cherokee in an animated way. Afterward, the chief said, "I was just agreeing with Oak that tracking painters ain't as easy as hunting bears, but for a fact, we must go after 'em and right soon. Eph Coward possesses some dogs 'specially bred to track long tails. I'll go down and talk to Eph and see about commencing a hunt right away."

"You're not going to collaborate with that sour mash moonshiner and his bunch of infidels are you?" Gilda Golden-feather said, nearly spitting out her words.

"Well now, mother," he replied sweetly, "at a time like this, I'd just about do bid'ness with the devil, could he do us some good."

Merlin and Goliath Dan nodded in agreement.

"Folks," Talking Rock said suddenly, getting up and heading to the door. "We best be moving on; got to get home and look after our stock and secure them for the night. I'll let y'all know when the painter hunt will commence. Probably day after tomorrow. In the meantime, you'd better keep your rifles at ready and shut up your stock. These are not just wolves we're dealing with now."

Oak Tree, meanwhile, went outside, got a ladder and brought down the panther tail. He handed it to Talking Rock. "My Lord! " The chief said, stretching it out. "That thing must be a yard long! Don't let Su-ta'li see it. She might faint."

"I take home," Oak Tree said and Talking Rock handed it back to him. He looped it over his rifle arm as he walked off toward his home near the mill.

The following day, Talking Rock let me go with him and Oak Tree down to see Ephraim Coward. I didn't let on what all I knew about the moonshiner. Of course, when Gu'li and I spied on him and his family, we saw them only from a distance.

Goodness yelped and ran off into the woods. I was surprised that Talking Rock would let her run loose with the chance that a long tail could get her like it did Mercy. Then I remembered that the big cats don't rove much of a day.

When we got in hollering range of Eph's place, Talking Rock yelled a loud "haaa-loooo." The old man came straight out of his house. He was right friendly and invited everyone in. He was smoking a corncob pipe and I noticed that his fluffy white sideburns came way down on the sides of his face.

He was a lot bigger around in the chest than I remembered him from afar when we spied on him, and his arms and chest appeared to be packed with hard muscles. His face, though, was the same apple red color that I recalled from before. Talking Rock told me later the ruddy look was due to his Scottish heritage. On the other hand, his eyes gleamed the bluest I'd ever seen in a person's eyes.

"So the hollerin' thangs got to your place too, eh?" Eph said.

"Yes indeed," Talking Rock said. "Two long tails. Large and yellow. They killed some of my chickens and even got my hound dog, Mercy."

"You lost Mercy? I'm awful sorry to hear that. You mean your dogs stood up to them long tail cats?"

"Sure did. They were protecting our home. But I guess Goodness will be right shy now that Mercy was killed and carried away."

"That's a everlastin' shame to lose one of your dogs," Eph said.

"Did y'all hear that one of the painters tried to paw through Su-ta'li's roof last night? And with her and the boys inside."

"Did he get in?"

"No, I shot at him; didn't kill him but I shot off his tail. T'san-us'di here was in the loft with a flintlock, and was preparing to shoot him through a hole in the shingles."

"Do tell."

✯ ✯ ✯

"Eph, I know you have the right dogs to hunt long tails."

"You're right, Talking Rock. We've bred us some really mean dogs that can shore track 'em down."

He took us down to his dog pens and showed us his Black and Tans, his long-legged, deep-throated hounds that he used to hunt deer, possums and raccoons, and his famed Plott bear dogs. In a separate area, Eph took us to the pen holding his vicious panther dogs.

"They're half wolf and half Indian cur," he said, showing us one he called Shadrack. He was slick, black and ugly looking, with a vicious snarl and a powerful jaw. In the same pen was his brother, Meshak. A third one, Abednego, had died of pneumonia.

"What if those wolf dogs smelled a coon or a bear?"

"Now Talking Rock, you ought to know better than ask a fool question lak that," Eph said. Changing the subject quickly, Talking Rock said, "Eph, we were wondering if you would be able to help us on a painter hunt."

"Why shore, Talking Rock. Be mor'n happy to hep you. My boys Lige and Faron could go with us; they got strong legs and they know how to run these dogs. When do you want to go?"

"Maybe day after tomorrow."

"That would work out fine. We'll come to your place with our wagon and plenty of provisions."

We headed back home in a happy frame. As we neared our cabin Talking Rock told me to start getting my duds ready. "*You mean you're gon'a let me go?*" I said.

"Why not, boy? You need to learn sometime. And I haven't even taken you on that promised bear hunt yet."

"Thank you, oh, thank you, sir," I said, shaking his hand high up and down.

"My pleasure, boy. Only one or two things I ask of you, T'san: Stay away from waterfalls and ivy slicks and watch out for rattlesnakes crawling into their winter homes under rocks."

To which I said I would abide by his every rule. Then I asked, right out of the blue, "What about Gu'li?"

"What about him?" he said.

"Can he go, too?"

He gave me that long and silent Indian stare of his and then he said, after a long pause, "You think you could look after him?"

"*Yes sir, I sure could!*"

"All right then, it's settled. But I want y'all to mind me all the time and stay pert and keep yourself and Gu'li close at hand, but out of the way."

"You'll not need to worry about us a single minute, Talking Rock."

I guess he saw the wide grin covering my face. I was grinning in my mind, too. I could hardly wait to visit Gu'li to break the news. He'd be mighty proud to learn that I worked a miracle to get him aboard on the big hunt. I ran back home in a whoop.

# CHAPTER FOURTEEN

## Going After the Long Tails

The next morning, the smell of roasting chestnuts greeted me when I walked into Wa-gu'li's cabin. He offered me a cup of hot chestnuts and told me to make myself at home at the cona-han'ee pot. Both warmed me all the way down to the bottom of my belly. As I stood there near the big fireplace and loft ladder I well remembered the awful night before.

Su-ta'li was in a brighter frame of mind than during the panther scare, but I was about to bust trying to contain my big news. Gu'li noticed it right off.

"What are you holding back, T'san?" he asked.

"Why do you think I'm holding something back?"

"Just the proud way you walked in. That and your wild grin. You haven't stopped grinning since you came through the door."

"Gu'li, you won't believe it; Talking Rock is inviting us to join the panther hunt."

Gu'li's eyebrows arched into a mountain of joy and he broke into a big smile.

"*You and me?*" he asked. "*We'll go with the crowd hunting the long tails?*"

"Cross my heart and hope to die. Straight from Talking Rock's mouth."

"*Whoopeeee!*"

We danced a jig around the room and started talking about what we would need to take with us.

"Who else is going?"

"Eph Coward and two of his boys, plus Goliath Dan and Oak Tree."

I was taken aback when Su-ta'li began staring at us in the strange Indian manner.

"What do you think of it, ma'am?" I asked. She didn't look too happy.

"You boys take a seat, and let me tell you a story," she said as she eased into her rocking chair. "It happened many years ago and it involved you and me, Little Fox."

"What are you talking about, Ma?" Gu'li asked.

"I've never told you about it, my son, but when you were an infant child, before you could walk, we encountered a painter in the remote mountains. I was walking over to the cabin of my grandfather, Bear-at-Home. It was a cold day and I had you wrapped in a blanket and strapped you on my back.

"I got within a mile of grandpa's cabin, walking a trail besides Noon-toot'lee Creek.

"All at once, from up on the ridge, here came this awful scream. It sounded like a giant woman warrior going into battle; it had an awful deep-throated whine to it, and oh, so loud!

"I was shaken something awful. Even my fice dog Dandy got nervous and curled his tail underneath him and started whining. I yelled for grandpa and started running toward his cabin.

"Every time I yelled, the long tail screamed back, like an echo almost. From his howls and growls, I could tell he was getting closer and closer. It got worse with every step I took. I ran faster, with Dandy running beside me. Then I looked over to the right and saw him; he was a painter for sure, a big yellow cat. He was trotting upon the ridge right alongside us, swishing his long tail behind him and slapping it into the ground ever so often—plop, plop, plop. I stepped into a crevice and almost lost my footing. Thank the Great Spirit I got back on my feet and was able to continue running.

"Finally I got within sight of Bear-at-Home's cabin, and I yelled again. Grandpa heard me and rushed out with his rifle.

"*A long tail's after us, Grandpa!*" I yelled, "*right there on the ridge.*"

"He fired up that way and the big cat scooted off in

a hurry. I dashed into the house, put you down near the warm fire and and helped Grandpa bolt the door."

There was a moment of silence and then she resumed her story:

"I see that your heart is set to go on the painter hunt, my son," she said. "I can't stop you. But I'll be praying for you all the time you're gone and I suggest that you and Jon-boy should be praying throughout that hunt, a constant prayer."

As I walked back home the snow was coming down hard and it was turning colder by the minute. The cloudy sky had darkened and the winds were rising. But I kept thinking about Su-ta'li's account and I wondered why an animal of the forest would want to attack someone just walking along like that. Maybe he thought he could get an easy supper, particularly with the baby boy. I was surely glad that Gu'li and his ma got away from the hungry panther.

I'd heard stories about the tawny panthers that nobody much ever saw because they move around mostly in the dark of night.

Talking Rock told me later that the creatures had a mysterious past. "Years ago the Cherokees looked up to long tails," he said. "They called them 'the Cats of God,' and they wanted their infant boys to sleep on panther skins so they would take on the animal's speed, strength and smartness, and of course his ability to leap fast and high."

"What about baby girls?" I asked.

"They have had a different idea about infant females. Cherokee mothers usually laid their infant girls down on soft sheepskin, aiming for them to grow up to be gentle and sweet, yet strong."

Talking Rock, Gu'li and I discussed provisions for the trip. "We'll need to prepare to stay out for at least three days and nights," the chief said. "I'd advise you both to wear at least three layers of clothes plus deerskin boots. Your mothers should be able to get you prepared real good."

"I'll need to carry a rifle, won't I?"

"Of course."

"But I really don't know how to shoot."

"You don't? I saw you hanging up that muzzle loader at Su-ta'li's last night."

"That was the rifle Guli's pa used in the Battle of Horse-shoe Bend. But I've never fired a rifle in my life."

"I'll get Conrad Carreker to teach you."

That afternoon, I went back home and told Ma about our upcoming hunt. She was concerned but gave her permission. Mister Carreker arrived and had me pull out my Pa's old muzzle loader. I didn't feel comfortable with it at first. It was awful heavy.

"Main thing, T'san," he said, "is to be steady with your hands. And if you can find a tree limb or some-such to lay your barrel on, that'll help you steady your aim."

After a little bit, I got accustomed to holding the piece, and he set up a broken clay mug on a log and told me to shoot at it. I took plenty of time, then squeezed the flint lock trigger. The jolt knocked me back against a pine tree, but I busted the mug to smithereens. He slapped me on the shoulder, and said, "Excellent! Your Pa would've been real proud of you, Jon-boy."

Following another overnight snowfall, the next day dawned bright and clear and Eph Coward's son, Faron, came up to say they would be ready to start out later in the day, and sure enough, about mid morning, we heard the ringing of bells and we knew the Coward crowd was getting near. When we went outside, the old man was walking up, in front of his mules that were carrying bells on their harness!

"*Mornin' fellers!*" he yelled.

Everybody said hello.

"Well sir, winter has done got hyar! " he said, speaking in a loud voice to one and all. Cold vapors rose from his mouth as he talked, and I could see little icicles had formed on the hairs sticking out of his nose. He was unusually jovial and his face was flushed. I guessed he had gotten into some of his favorite beverages on his way here.

"Air you fellers ready for the hunt?" he yelled again with a grin. Everybody nodded and Talking Rock said, "We sure are, Eph." Coming up also was Lige, Eph's oldest son, leading two pack mules, their bells jingling, and a steer wagon loaded down with camp gear including four long rifles, cooking gear, plus a bunch of grub including a big slab of side meat.

Bringing up the rear was Faron, Eph's redheaded middle son, who held the two black wolf dogs on chains with deer-gut muzzles around their mouths.

"Eph, looks like you're aiming to get you a long tail or two!" Talking Rock said.

"Ay Goddddd, Talking Rock, if we don't bring us one back we'll shore be caught tryin'."

"You got a purty good idee where them hollering thangs are denned, do ye,?"

"The way Oak Tree figures it they're way up on Fain Mountain, this side of the Nan'ta-ha'lee range. I'm persuaded they may have their den back up in some of those rock ledges."

"Well I'm ready to git started out if y'all are."

Our little caravan got moving, with Talking Rock and Eph Coward in the lead, followed by Gu'li and me and Goliath Dan plus the Coward boys with the mules, the steer wagon and the dogs. It was freezing cold but the snowfall had about stopped.

Oak Tree was waiting for us at his place. Eph Coward gave Oak a Cherokee arm shake, and put him up front. "He knows this country like the back of his hand," Eph told Talking Rock, "so he'll be our point man."

We walked for three hours, but Oak Tree would stop ever so often to call our attention to some oddity of the forest. He pointed to a red-shoulder hawk that was perched high atop a dead pine.

"Hawk seekin' dinner," Oak said. "Mebbe child rabbit."

Sometime later, as we stopped for a short break, Gu'li linked for me when I asked Oak Tree, "What about those tiny birds flitting around the trees and trilling like a bell?"

"Oh, I know about those," Gu'li spoke up before Oak Tree got a chance to reply. "They're black-eyed snow birds from up north and they're called Tu-ti'yi, snow birds. They look like sparrows but you can tell they're snowbirds because they have pink bills and white tails."

"That right," Oak Tree said.

The long shadows of late afternoon were evident when we reached Wildcat Creek.

"This here will make us a good camp site," Eph said after walking around a bit and noticing it was near a lively stream. The snowfall had stopped and we got busy cutting down saplings to make lean-tos. Gu'li and I would have one, Eph and the Coward boys another, and Oak Tree and Talking Rock would share a bigger one with Goliath Dan.

"Maybe we ort to shoot us a possum for supper!" the old man laughed in jest, as he started a roaring fire in the middle of our camp site. What he did cook was fast and tasty, cutting a hunk from his slab of bacon, slicing it up and slapping the thick slices into a big frying pan. The smell of that, plus the biscuits he put in another pan, gave everyone a powerful appetite.

While that was going on the Coward sons started digging holes. They set up two posts and hung up a pot in the middle. "We'll bile us up a squirrel stew overnight," Faron said, "so we'll have us somethin' that'll stick to our ribs in the mornin'."

By the time Gu'li and I got through cutting saplings for our lean-to, and fixed up a network of limbs and pine needles for the roof and floor, the smell of the bacon and biscuits sharpened our hunger pangs, and we got in the line.

"Eat up good, boys," Eph said, "'cause you'un's gonna have some steep climbin' to do tomorrey, especially do we track the catty-mounts up to their den. Ain't that the truth of it, Oak Tree?"

"That right," Oak said.

Supper passed fast. Everyone cleaned out their tin plates and came up for seconds. Afterward, Eph pulled out his corncob pipe and lit it, and Goliath Dan cut off another chew of tobacco and took a seat on a dead log.

I'd been aching to get a chance to talk a bit to Oak Tree and, since we had a lull in the conversation, he agreed to some questions, and Gu'li said he'd be our linkster.

On my first question, I asked Oak about hunting in his younger years.

"When reach twenty-two winters me take likin' to Laughin'gal," he said, "and go on hunt. Bring home twenty deer that winter plus beavers, squirrels, rabbits."

"Did you tan and sell those hides?"

"Yass. With twelve skins, me buy petticoat for Laughin'gal. Then she marry me!"

We all laughed about that and Oak Tree joined in the laughing.

He remembered how panthers back then would attack their prey by jumping from tree limbs. "Painters kill baby horses that way," he said. "Big horses escape, get bloody claw marks on back."

I changed the subject and asked Oak if he ever used blood root.

"Yass, many times; blood root help if rattlesnake bite."

"I guess that's why people tell me they've never heard of any Cherokee dying of a snake bite!" I said.

"That's true," Gu'li said. "I can verify that old saying."

"When go in woods," Oak said, "we carry snake root in shot patch tied on leg. If rattler strike we chew blood root and rub root on bite."

"It worked, did it?" I asked.

"Always," Oak replied.

"Growing up, what was your biggest wish as a boy?" I asked

"Wish to shoot bow and arrow good as big brother. One day shoot down squirrel from poplar tree top. Big brother say, 'GOOD.'"

"Tell us of some thunderstorm memories."

"During Thunder Moon, big winds rain come from skies. Mothers hold dogs up in air to stop lightning, thunder."

Talking Rock broke in. "Our conjurer priests back then had a saying that the first loud thunder means that our Great Spirit is breaking the back of the winter."

I asked Oak Tree about his favorite food.

"Turtle soup. Mother make sweet turtle soup."

With Gu'li continuing to linkster, Oak recalled bringing home a snapping turtle one time. As usual, he said, his mother laid the turtle upside down on a tree stump and chopped his head off with an axe. Oak said his dog Shadow came sniffing around the head up close. The turtle head jumped up and locked onto Shadow's nose and stuck there for many hours.

"Feel sorry for Shadow," Oak said. "She run around crazy, dives in creek but turtle head stick on nose."

Eph spoke up to say, "We had an old saying that a snapping turtle wouldn't turn loose until it thundered."

Oak said, "No thunder that day. But turtle head jump off Shadow at sundown. Shadow so happy she climb up and kiss me on face."

As we turned in for the night, nobody had much to say about what was coming up in the morning. But it was on everyone's mind. I knew it was on my mind in a big way as I got into my sleeping bag, and I couldn't wait to get out there on Fain Mountain.

As I was going to sleep I could hear the howling of wolves nearby.

# CHAPTER FIFTEEN

## Shootout at Fain Mountain

Wa-gu'li woke me up at first light and, when I got my eyes open, I could see Eph Coward had a fire roaring and coffee boiling. It was right nippy out and I noticed that we'd had a light snow overnight.

Eph checked with his son about feeding the dogs. "Be shore and give them plenty of rations a'fore we head out," he told Faron.

"I've already laid out a pile of corn bread," Faron said, "along with a squirrel a'piece that we shot yesterday that I cooked up for 'em."

"That ort to do."

Talking Rock wondered if the dogs were being overfed.

"You don't want to feed 'em too much, do you, Eph? You want them to be hungry hunting the long tails, don't you?"

"Wal now, some folks starve their dogs a'fore a hunt, lak this'un, but I don't believe in it. I reckon if you expect your dogs to do their best for you on a hunt, that's the very time he needs all the energy he can get."

"You have a point there, Eph."

We ate us a mess of Eph's squirrel stew and drank his strong coffee. They both hit the spot, and, as Faron had predicted the night before, the stew gave us a good start for the day.

As we were getting ready to get started toward Fain Mountain, Faron and Lige brought up Shadrack and Meshak on chain leads and I saw up close their wide-apart eyes, their powerful jaws, and their long, vicious teeth. Their middles looked mighty muscular, too.

Oak Tree tried to pet Meshak, but the dog growled and bared his teeth.

"It's dangerous for a stranger to pet these rascals," Faron said as he pulled the dog back and muzzled him. "They can bite your hand off."

Eph told us to prepare for some fierce climbing. But he never revealed how to climb a mountain in cold weather. After we started out, the winds began howling as they swept down from the mountain. It reminded me of a Bible passage my pa used to quote from the book of John, where

Jesus tells about the wind blowing:

> *"You can hear its sound but you cannot*
> *tell where it comes from and where it's going.*
> *So it is with everyone born of the spirit."*

The storm didn't let up, but after we reached a plateau two hours later on the side of Fain mountain, Oak Tree discovered a big cave that slanted way back into the mountainside. "Be good stop," Oak said.

We piled right in, being grateful to get out of sleet that had commenced and was peppering our faces like pine needles. There was plenty of room for the whole bunch of us, including the dogs. A huge rock overhang shielded us from most of the elements, and Oak got a little fire started that we gathered around, two or three at a time.

We dozed for a while but I woke up fast when the dogs started barking loud and fierce, pulling Faron and Lige deep into the dark cave.

"Turn the dogs loose, boys," Eph yelled. "Let 'em go investigate. Somethin' must have come in from the other end!"

We could hear the wolf dogs tearing loose and racing into the darkness.

Goliath Dan found a long piece of heart pine and lit it to make a torch. He led the way into the cave with the rest of us following behind.

I noticed Eph getting his rifle primed and ready. I decided to do the same thing, just in case, filling my flintlock rifle with black powder and shot from the third layer inside my deerskin jacket. The tunnel roared with frenzied howling and Oak Tree and Eph swung their guns toward whatever it was causing the loud ruckus.

Goliath Dan raised his torch and Eph yelled, "Lord have mercy, fellers, look what we have here! "

What we saw was a black bear that had walked in from the snowstorm and was fighting off a panther, which apparently had come in for the same reason. On top of it all, the two dogs were tangling with the mountain lion right there in the middle of it all.

"I'd like to shoot both of 'em," Eph laughed, "but I'm a'feared I might hit one of my dogs."

In the meantime, the long tail started to turn away, but he didn't get far. Oak Tree's rifle blast brought him down.

The dogs started chewing up on the dying panther, leaving the bear standing up on his hind legs all alone, right there in front of us. Eph's gun went off, but the slug only grazed the bear's left shoulder and spun him around. The big old bear came up fighting mad and started toward us in an angry, slobbering rage. Everybody started backing up fast, me included.

"*Git out of the way, Dan!*" Eph yelled. "*That bar's a'comin' straight atter ye.*"

Dan turned his torch into a sword and his first swing singed the bear's right ear and slowed him down a bit. I pulled up my old muzzle loader and decided to shoot. I took a quick aim and pulled the trigger. The bear toppled over right at Eph Coward's feet.

*"You hit him, Jon-boy!"* Talking Rock yelled, using my old name. *"You got him right through the heart. Great shot!"*

About that time, Dan's torch went out and there we were, deep in the dark cave, along with a dead panther, a dead bear, two crazy wolf dogs and no light. On top of that, Pa's old gun had knocked me down and I was sprawled out flat on my back there in the dark cave, a few feet from the dead bear.

"We in pickle," Oak Tree yelled from somewhere in the dark.

"Shore are, Oak," Eph laughed from the other side of the tunnel, as only he can laugh, and everybody started laughing.

"At least we're alive," Gu'li spoke out, laughing himself.

"Glory be!" Goliath Dan replied.

"And praise the Lord," I said from my prone position. Gu'li heard me and felt around, reached down and helped me get up.

"Keep the dogs from tearin' up that painter skin," Eph yelled back to his boys.

"We've got 'em both muzzled and on chains," Lige hollered back.

Goliath Dan got another torch lit, but it took Eph, Talking Rock and Oak Tree a good while to drag out the two carcasses.

At the cave entrance, we were happy to see that the sleet

and snow had stopped and that light was coming down from the cloud-scattered sky.

"Let's get these beasts skinned," Eph Coward said, and he and Dan and Oak Tree lifted them up, one at a time, and took them out front.

"I think we can use our ropes to hang the painter on that poplar limb right there," Eph said. So, once they got the first carcass up on ropes, they started skinning the beast. They did the same for the bear carcass.

"I believe we can leave these carcasses hanging right here for a few hours," Talking Rock said.

"Shore can," Eph replied. "They'll be safe in this hyar freezing weather until we can get our mules out here to haul 'em back to our base camp."

After they skinned the bear, I could see that Eph was thinking ahead about the delicious bear meat. "That'll make some good eatin'," he said, "to say nothin' of the oil we can get from the painter. Dessie Mae can use it for her cookin' and for our lamps."

"*Me shot painter!*" Oak Tree protested, pleading in a soft but determined voice. "*Me like painter meat. Laugh'n-gal cook painter oil!*"

"Oak," I asked, "what will you do with panther oil?"

"Rub me elbows. . .knees. . .fingers." I learned later that Oak was plagued with painful arthritis in his joints and that panther oil was the best thing to bring him relief on a cold night.

After hearing that, Eph Coward said he'd be mighty happy to give all the panther meat to the beloved old full-blood.

Before we left the cave, Eph showed off the panther skin, laying it out on the ground for all to see, along with the bear skin.

"That's a mighty big catamount, Oak," Talking Rock said, "and you shot him right in the side of the head. You're a mighty good shot."

"*Wadan*," Oak said. (thank you).

"And did y'all notice?" Gu'li asked. "The cat's tail is missing!"

"*It is?*" I yelled. "*That must be the rascal that tried to claw his way into Su-ta'li's roof that night, with me right there under him in the loft!*"

"Shore is, T'san," Talking Rock laughed, looking up at the cat's tailless skin. "Yes sir, he's the scoundrel that lost his tail to my old Betsy."

The next morning after breakfast at our camp site, Faron and Lige Coward arrived with the two carcasses strapped on the mules, and they transferred them to the wagon for the return trip. The weather had improved so much the rest of us decided to walk straight home behind the wagon.

All the way back, our crowd could talk of nothing but the exciting day in the cave. Goliath Dan patted me on the back again and Gu'li said, "T'san-us'di, you're going to become known as '*The Hi-wass'ee hero: The young man who shot a bear while out on a panther hunt!'"*

I just smiled a bit, but my heart was busting with pride and it was difficult suppressing a big grin.

The next day, Faron Coward drove up in their wagon and knocked on Talking Rock's door. The chief invited him in.

"Pa wanted me to come bring y'all some of the meat that came from the bear the young man shot," he said.

"That's mighty kind of you," Talking Rock said, and then hollered for me to come over from next door and accept it, which I did, thanking Faron for the kind gesture.

"I've got somethin' else for you, young man," Faron said. He walked back to his wagon, and returned with the big bear skin.

"Pa wanted you to have this skin. You'll have to get Oak Tree to tan it for you. You might get a nice coat out of it."

I was speechless, and I guess he noticed I had a tear in my eye. But I shook Faron's hand like a man and told him to take back to his father my most sincere and heartfelt thanks.

I couldn't wait to show it off to all my friends, starting with Gu'li and Ma.

# CHAPTER SIXTEEN

### Federal Agents Cause a Near Riot, and a Visit with Chief White Path

It's amazing how things can suddenly change a person's life. Since our big hunt at Fain Mountain, the Cherokees and the missionary folks have been treating me like I'm a wonderful man. I couldn't believe it when my friend Oak Tree started calling me "Mister T'san."

The best upshot of that bear-kill was that it pumped up my spirits as never before. Throughout my life, I'd had doubts about myself. It's a secret I've kept to myself; I never mentioned it to Ma and Pa and not even to my buddy Gu'li.

As a result, after bringing down the black bear, I got to

thinking hard about my new situation in life. It has had me worried, in a way. I felt the need to talk it over with someone and my first thought was Missionary Merlin. He's such a level-headed fellow and well educated. So at the first chance, I brought up the subject with him.

"Well T'san," he told me, "you're growing up fast and it's wonderful that you possess this increased feeling of self-acceptance following what I would call something of an inferiority complex. Many young people are plagued with such doubts and it's good that you're breaking free of that. Our Lord teaches us that we must love ourselves before we can love other people. Many people never in their entire lives ever reach such a level of self confidence as you now possess. So you are a very blessed person indeed.

"On the other hand, T'san, the Good Book also tells us that a man should not turn haughty and think more highly of himself than he ought to. That could apply to you if you don't watch out."

"Well, what should I do, Merlin?" I asked.

"First of all—and I think you're on a good start—is to accept yourself in a positive way and guard against conceit. In other words, avoid thinking of yourself as being better than others. Just continue to love people as they are and consider them to be on the same level as yourself, not below you and not above you."

"Are you saying I need to show more humility along with self-assurance?" I asked.

"Yes, that's a good way to put it. You might want to read your New Testament more often, and follow Paul's instructions for living a full life. He urges us to be positive in all our dealings with people, be they high or low. And as Jesus said, 'don't hide your light in a basket,' but at the same time, practice humility without guile in all relationships."

I went away from that meeting with a new understanding of myself and I headed straight to Gu'li's place. I let him know about meeting with Merlin and we started talking about what we should be planning to do with the rest of our lives.

"We're both moving toward manhood," Guli said, "and we probably need to set some goals for ourselves. For myself, I would like dedicate myself to helping the Cherokee Nation."

"Maybe that should be my mission in life also," I said. "Talking Rock told me yesterday that the Georgia leaders at Milledgeville are aligned with President Jackson in trying to uproot Cherokees from their homes and to move everyone beyond the Mississippi."

"That's what I've been hearing, too," he said.

The situation became real to us the following day, when two agents of the Federal Government rode into our valley and started passing out talking leaves to folks all around. Several Cherokees ran up to the mission with copies. About that time, the two men rode up the trail to the mission. Talking Rock went out to meet them.

"What are you men doing here?"

"We don't mean to intrude, sir," the first uniformed officer replied from atop his horse, taking off his hat. "We're from Washington City and we're representing President Jackson. We just want to inform your people about the advantages of moving west. Ar-kan'saw is a beautiful, wide open country with plenty of fertile land and rivers galore that your people would find enjoyable as a safe new place to live and work."

"You have no right to barge into our nation like this," Talking Rock said. "Did you get permission from anyone down in our capital of New E-cho'ta to roam around our country like this?" His answer was in the negative.

Meantime, a crowd started gathering. Some of the men brought out their flintlock rifles from the 1814 Horseshoe Bend battle and the situation became tense.

"I suggest you take your leaflets back to Washington City before you get hurt around here," Talking Rock said, "and tell that renegade turncoat of a president that we have no interest in or intention to move west. Our people would rather die than leave behind our homes here in this country and the sacred bones of our ancestors."

One of the Cherokees yelled out, "Jackson is a *u–tlo'nas'de* (hypocrite) and a *de'li* (skunk)," drawing other angry yells from the crowd.

The two spurred their horses and made a hasty retreat. As they were leaving, Talking Rock addressed the crowd:

"Brothers and sisters, I regret to say we're now engaged in a war with the United States of America and the nearby state of Georgia. I want to advise you men to grease up your rifles and get them in shape to use. And be sure to store up plenty of bullets and gunpowder."

As we walked back down the trail, Gu'li and I were both furious.

"It's a shame that Andrew Jackson has turned his back against us," Gu'li said. "Just a decade ago, our Cherokee hero, Major Ridge, at Jackson's request, recruited more than 500 of our warriors, and formed a Cherokee unit to help Jackson defeat the Red Sticks over in Al-a'bam'a."

"That was in eighteen and fourteen," he added. "Immediately after that victory on the bend of the Tal-la'poo'sa River, Jackson heaped high praise on our fighters for their help. Many of our warriors died in that battle, including my dear father, and scores were wounded. So I have a terrible pain in my heart hearing stories about Jackson's turnaround."

"I feel for you, Gu'li," I said. "It galls me too that our President—now sitting up there in the catbird seat in Washington—could be so insensitive to the pleas of his old Cherokee allies.

"The worst part about it, Gu'li," I added, "is that our warriors may have helped him get elected president, since after that victory over the Red Sticks he went on to defeat the British in New Orleans, which led almost directly to his election to the White House."

We went over to our hideaway and talked a long time about how we might go about helping our nation in this time of trial.

A month later, with anger rising among the Cherokees in the valley, Gu'li, Merlin and I let it be known that we wanted to visit the Chief White Path who lives in El'i-ja, in the mountains of northeast Georgia.

"I hear that he is an influential mountain full-blood," I said. "We need to get his suggestions as how we can fight our new enemies."

"And besides that," Gu'li said, "White Path fought in the same Cherokee regiment with my dad in that battle at Horseshoe Bend. He might tell me something about how my father lost his life."

So, on an early morning in May the four of us left on horseback. It took us two days. We stopped overnight at Fighting Town, and the next morning we headed directly to El'i-ja, situated at the head of the Ku-sa'watt'ee River.

The day was dying into darkness when we arrived. "We're coming up to the river right now," Corn Silk yelled from in front. "Get ready to ford it." He spurred his horse into the knee-deep water and clattered smartly across. The rest of us followed behind without difficulty.

As our horses climbed the far bank, we came onto the village's festival grounds and were startled by what we saw. A crowd of young Indians, mostly boys, started running toward us, whooping and hollering, led by a feathered fellow atop a horse who was carrying a torch. It scared me at first, but Corn Silk quickly eased our minds.

"They're friendly," he said, "just coming out to greet us." They'd painted their faces and chests in all sorts of crazy patterns—red and white, yellow and blue—plus rings of red and black around their eyes. A few of the older men sported silver and gold rings hanging from their ears.

They clustered around Corn Silk's gelding, and the linkster jumped down and shook arms all around, patted some heads and hugged a few necks. I could see he was well-loved from previous visits, so I reckoned it was something of a sweet reunion. Corn Silk introduced us to the leader and we went through an arm shaking with him and several others.

The booming drumbeats in the distance got louder and we followed the torchbearer, riding our horses across the hard-packed grounds. Flames flickered from more torches, and suddenly we found ourselves being greeted by a multitude of folks—maybe the entire village—men, women and children of all sizes and descriptions, dancing and shouting. They swarmed all around us with warm smiles.

We heard later that White Path had invited people from all around, from Car-te'cay, Cherry Log, Mountain Town, Turnip Town and Tick'a-nett'ly. Before we knew it, the throng had swelled to maybe two hundred head. The women were dressed out in red, yellow and blue calico skirts and blouses and beautifully-beaded moccasins. They flaunted their lustrous black hair, rolled up in swirls on top. Several carried pebble-filled turtle shells attached to their ankles. They would be dancing later, Corn Silk told us.

We jumped down and turned our horses over to some young lads. The torch bearer led us and the whole multitude toward a big tent that was circled by more torches topping tall poles. In the middle blazed a lively fire that lit up the darkening night in an almost romantic way. Over to the right stood a building constructed of vertical poles. "That's the El'i-ja Town House," Corn Silk said proudly.

About that time, a tall, smiling Indian came striding out of the tent, light on his moccasins, and stretched his arms open wide. He was carrying a wand topped with white and black eagle feathers. I heard later that they'd come from eagles he'd shot himself. Three shiny eagle feathers topped his head and silver bands glittered on his arms. Around his neck hung a necklace of shells.

"That's Chief White Path," Corn Silk said quietly. I had figured as much. His head was covered with a shock of silver hair. Handing off his eagle wand to an aide, the chief grabbed Corn Silk's hands and then Merlin's and held them high in a gesture of friendship.

"*You have come,*" he said in a deep booming voice in Cherokee. "*It is good.*"

Then he addressed his villagers, with Corn Silk doing the linkstering.

"My brothers, I don't hold many Una'kas in high regard. Our experience tells us most are mean, greedy and contentious, and yes, in some cases they are liars and cheats, often seeking not our friendship but our land. So I am happy to introduce a different type Una'ka who has come into our midst. Born in Scotland, he lived for some time in Charleston, where he got his education, and now he is a missionary in the Hi'wass-ee Valley. And, while he has the skin of a European paleface, he possesses the soul of an Indian, and he has become a good friend to the Chero-kees—Missionary Merlin Montgomery!"

The crowd roared its welcome. I reckoned that Corn Silk must have sent some talking leaves to White Path in advance, telling him all about Merlin.

"And of course," White Path said, "you all know our friend, Corn Silk, who is Brother Merlin's linkster and guide."

The throng whooped, stomped their feet and clapped their hands.

"And these two young men are his friends, T'san-us'di and Wa-gu'li."

We received a light smattering of hand claps and we clapped back.

White Path led us to our deerskin seats around the fire, underneath the big tent. The chief took the bearskin seat in the middle, and motioned for us to sit beside him, with Corn Silk on his left, since he would be the linkster, and on the other side, Merlin and me and Gu'li.

The first thing White Path did was to pull out his big clay pipe with the long stem and fill it with tobacco. Then, one of his people ran up with a hot coal. After taking a puff, he handed it over to Merlin, who followed suit, and the pipe was passed on to Corn Silk and then back to White Path.

"Now we shall eat," White Path said, signaling his people

to start bringing out the food. "Thank goodness," Merlin whispered. "I'm famished. I hope they've killed the fatted calf."

"I hear it's fatted beavers," Corn Silk said with a wry grin.

"*Beavers?*" Merlin replied, a bit disappointed.

"Now don't give up just yet, Brother Merlin," Corn Silk said. "Wild meat can be right tasty, if cooked properly. Cherokees par boil them first, then bake them with onions in a Dutch Oven over a fire, and sometimes they proceed to fry them in bear's oil."

Brimming gourds of soup came out first. Merlin gulped his down quickly.

"Delicious, Corn Silk, just delicious! Tell me, what kind of soup is it?"

"It's yellow jacket soup."

Merlin laid down his spoon with his mouth hanging open.

"Merlin, you're not back in Charleston," Corn Silk said. "This is one of the Cherokees' cherished delicacies. They dig up nests of yellow jacket grubs from the ground early in the spring, whole combs of them. Then they toast them at the fire place, following which they chop up the browned grubs and and cook them in bear grease. And as you have now learned, the soup is delicious, with a little salt added."

"My friends on Meeting Street in Charleston will never

believe it," Merlin said, "but I must confess this soup was rather tasty."

"We liked it, too," I said. Of course, I realized it was routine food for Gu'li.

Next came baskets of roasted beaver along with corn cakes fried in hickory nut oil, with bear's oil on the side. I dipped a hunk of the meat in the oil and chomped down. Merlin did the same.

"This beaver is not bad," Merlin said. "In fact, it's rather delicious."

The last course—persimmon pudding and wild honey, along with possum grape wine—was brought out. Most delicious, we all agreed.

Afterward, we went up to thank the chief for the warm welcome and delicious dinner, and Gu'li asked him if he perhaps had met up with his father, Jim Eagle, in the 1814 battle against the Creek Red Sticks in Ala-ba'ma.

"Oh yes, Wa-gu'li," White Path answered. "I knew Jim Eagle very well. He was in my company and I first got to know him during the initial fighting farther north in Al-a'bam'a before the decisive final battle at Horseshoe Bend—*To-ho'pe'ka* they called it.

"I was distressed when Jim lost his life in that battle," White Path said. "The fight lasted all day; Jim and I had gone with Major Ridge's group in circling around in a pincer movement to the back side of the river bend. We rode canoes across the river and battled the Red Sticks attempting to escape from the main battle scene. I saw your father engaged in a hand-to-hand-struggle there in the river.

Later, he died instantly when hit by a Red Stick bullet. He fell immediately in the water and I helped pull his body out. The day after the battle, we buried him in the woods nearby with the other deceased Cherokees."

Into the night, a rousing Eagle Tail stomp dance got under way nearby, with the women rattling turtle shells attached to their feet and circling the fire, followed by the men. Gul'i and I were taken by what Corn Silk called pantomimes. On past midnight, the party turned wild when the men and women started pulling off their western style dresses and coats and hats and throwing them into the fire. Of course, many were drinking white whiskey that added to their angry passion.

"What's going on?" I asked Corn Silk.

"These mountain Indians have become angered anew in recent days about removal talk from Andrew Jackson's agents, and are following their conjurer priest calls to abandon white ways and return to the traditions of their fathers."

Gu'li and I asked Corn Silk for more details.

"I understand that it started with fiery talks by their full-blood priests in all these villages around here, urging them to become true Indians again.

"You'll hear from White Path tomorrow," Corn Silk said, "but he is increasingly agitated these days, furious that that the governor of Georgia has launched an all-out assault on the Cherokee Nation along with President Jackson."

We went to bed with many questions in our minds, but we were looking forward to having some time with White Path in the morning.

"My name is *Nunna'hi-Sune'ga*," the chief told us the next morning, "but our people call me White Path since I have tried to travel a path of peace, in contrast to the red path of blood and violence and war. Of course, I was happy to answer Major Ridge's appeal to join in fighting the Creek Red Sticks in Al-a'bam'a."

We were out on White Path's front porch and yard. He had invited us to join him there after enjoying a con'a-han'ee breakfast. Corn Silk was linkstering, as usual.

White Path spoke of his pride in being a "mountain full-blood," having been born here in the Cherokee mountains, within the chartered limits of northeast Georgia.

When he was a young man, he told us, he exchanged marriage vows with Lo'ni of the Wolf Clan and gave her a venison ham as a pledge of providing meat for their table. She, in turn, gave him an ear of corn, showing her ability to raise food crops such as beans, squash and corn.

"I was born right near here, at Turnip Town. My greater father told me that from the early days, El'i-ja was known as the green valley, where the earth is green. The Car-te'cay and El'i-ja Rivers come together here and their waters, in time of flooding, spread fertile soil across our bottom lands, insuring abundant harvests.

"From the time I was a small child," he continued, "I felt deeply that, among the Creator God's greatest gifts to his children here below, were the streams that caress our valley. I often considered how the El'i-ja and the Car-te'cay Rivers, chattering children in our Cherokee lore, swept down the western ridges of the Blue Ridge Divide, converging here in our valley to create the Ku'sa-watt'ee, the Big Man river—*Yun'wi Guna'hi'ti*—whose head is said to rest here in the mountains and whose feet lie in the lowlands near the sea."

He told how the waters cut briskly southwestward through the Cohuttas, carrying away his sins every day and those of other prayerful Cherokees, cutting a deep gorge through a limestone canyon, plunging down five hundred feet along a twelve-mile stretch in a churning onrush.

Farther down, he said, the wild river, adding the waters of Mountain Town Creek, Sala-co'a Creek, Indian Creek and Talking Rock Creek, suddenly turn gentle, spreading out to the wide banks in the Great Valley at Old Ku'sa Town. The smooth waters, he added, glide gently by several islands, and are so shallow that horses and people can easily ford the ankle-deep water.

"And to think that each of our big rivers begins with a quiet little spring," he said, "such as those found by the hundreds in our hills, where cold water sprouts sweetly from the earth."

Corn Silk told us later that White Path meditates often about these streams, all bearing Indian names, some

of them from the Creeks, who also occupied much of the
lands north of the Chatt-a'hoo'chee River in past centuries
and which he feels came from the hand of the Creator
God, *Yo'wah*, whose name is so sacred that no Cherokees
except the *Ad-hon'skee* priests are allowed to speak the word
out loud.

White Path told us that he continues to go to the water every morning as his forefathers did. He spends a lot
of time praying, Corn Silk said, followed by the ancient
purification tradition. Thus, even on the coldest of days,
he dashes into the icy waters of the El'i-ja River for his
morning prayers, then dashes to the *a'si* hot house, without
a whimper.

White Path gazed into the far distance and spoke of his
love for the Tick'a-nett'ly Bald to the east and Big Frog
Mountain and the long Co-hut'ta range on the west.

> *"Such wild grandeur we have all around us!" he said.*
> *"The mountains and valleys and streams, the animals*
> *and the plants. And the sun and the moon and the stars,*
> *a beautiful display of the Great Spirit's love for his humble*
> *children here below, and whose love is reflected in every*
> *living plant, animal and person."*

After a few moments of silence, White Path spoke up
again, changing the subject.

He confirmed the religious fervor that was spreading

across the Cherokee mountain country as reflected in the wild midnight dance.

"You saw the angry feeling of our people last night as they burned their modern clothes and pledged to return to the Cherokee life of our fathers. They are angry—as I am—with the Georgians in Milledgeville who are trying to destroy our nation and push our people out west. And, of course, they're angry at President Jackson, the ingrate turncoat.

"We lost a great ally when the British were defeated in the American Revolutionary War. But, I'm happy that most of the missionaries are on our side. And for this I am grateful to people such as our distinguished visitor, Merlin Montgomery.

"And our leaders, like John Ross, are in Washington City, trying to persuade American senators to help stop the foolish removal drive being led and abetted by our turncoat national president.

"But I must say in all honesty, our prospects don't look good. We must get our communities prepared to defend ourselves in case it comes to a war. So, I'm advising the chiefs in all our towns to start building up their stock of weapons and ammunition. I hope it doesn't come to war. But if it does, we must be prepared."

It was a sobering thought. As we left the next morning, we went straight back to our homes with heavy hearts.

# CHAPTER SEVENTEEN

## Merlin Tours the Valley

After returning from visiting Chief White Path, I was eager to help Cherokee leaders prepare for the coming battle with Georgia and their allies in Washington led by Andrew Jackson, the turncoat president. I thought immediately of Merlin. Surely he has some new ideas after after visiting Chief White Path. Lo and behold, when I walked out of our front door the next morning there was Merlin saddling up Alice, the mission horse.

"Where you going, Merlin?" I hollered.

"Up the valley to visit with a few Cherokee families. How's your mother, by the way?"

"She's still in a sickly way and I'm getting worried. She

has a croupy cough and she'll probably be in bed most of the morning. Su-ta'li will be coming this morning to care for her."

"I'll ask some of the old Cherokees what they might have to suggest in the way of root medicines," Merlin said. "I understand some of their medicine doctors favor elm bark."

I knew that Ma would be willing to try such a Cherokee "bitters" but not if she knew it contained as much as a tiny drop or two of ardent spirits.

This would be Merlin's first journey on his own without Corn Silk by his side, but he was fast learning the Cherokee tongue by study and by conversing with Cherokees possessing some knowledge of English.

I asked about Corn Silk. "He can't join me because he has a ball play today," Merlin said. "He'll be the star player for Hi-wass'ee."

Merlin had attempted to arrange a baptizing of Corn Silk some weeks earlier, but Preacher Paul wouldn't allow it.

"Never, never, never! " the head missionary had roared. "Not as long as Corn Silk engages in the ball play. It's blasphemous, because it fosters gambling and drinking and debauchery."

"Maybe Corn Silk could help us clean it up," Merlin suggested.

"The only way to deal with the nefarious ball play is to abolish it," Preacher Paul replied. "The ball play is an abomination in the eyes of God. We'll never Christianize the Cherokees until we eradicate the ball play."

I knew that Merlin had accepted the games as a Chero-kee fact of life, and, as a newcomer to the mission, he told me he was trying to look at the problem from the view-point of the Indians.

"We missionaries," he said, "should exploit the Chero-kees' love of the game by lovingly seeking to convert the players such as Corn Silk, and through them try to reduce and eventually eliminate the drinking and gambling that accompany the games."

As Merlin saddled up Alice, I asked him if I could go with him.

"I don't have room for you, Jon. I'll have Alice loaded down with gifts for the Indian children and boxes of talk-ing leaves Bible tracts."

"Hey, Merlin, you won't need to worry about me," I said. "I can ride Bullet, my Shetland pony." Talking Rock re-cently told me I could have Bullet if I would agree to take care of her, which I was happy to do so, including getting her fed and exercised every day.

"And besides having my own pony, Merlin, maybe I could fill in as your linkster. I've been learning a lot of Cherokee talk from Wa-gu'li."

After more pleading on my part, Merlin finally gave in. So I hurriedly saddled up my pony. His first destina-tion was at a village on the way to Gan'a-hee'da, where he would meet with some converts and spend the night with one of the local Indian families. On our way there I figured I might be able to ask him about the war looming between the white Una'ka Georgians and the Cherokees.

I was surprised by the number of youngsters who waved at the new missionary as we rode by. Talking Rock had told me that many children and their parents had come to like the young red head Scottish missionary from Charleston and his Indian duds.

Unlike Preacher Paul, who always went everywhere wearing a black suit and a black felt hat, Merlin started dressing more and more like the Indians. He hung a feather from his hair at first, a bright yellow one. And he wore moccasins, finding that his feet appreciated the change. The rest of his clothing was strictly Cherokee homespun, including deerskin pants.

"When the weather turns cold," he told me, "I plan to wear a deerskin jacket that Laugh'in-gal made for me, decorated with rawhide fringes on the sleeves."

The greatest stir in the missionary ranks came when Merlin took to wearing a bright yellow turban about his head much like some of the full-bloods. A trader sold him a yard of bright yellow calico and he created his own turban. The day Merlin showed up wearing the head piece, the head missionary nearly had a fit.

"Mister Montgomery! " Preacher Paul said, raising his

voice and pointing a bony index finger at Merlin.

"Yes, sir."

"What do you think you're doing?"

"I've made myself a Cherokee turban, sir."

"You can't be serious, young man."

"What better way to minister to our Cherokees than to dress as they do."

"Mister Montgomery, our national office would not approve of it. I'm afraid that headpiece is not in keeping with the dignity of our calling."

As always when wrought, Preacher Paul's face would turn crimson red, and he would start chewing his tongue. On such occasions, the old missionary could be counted on to give his audience an awful tongue-lashing.

"It's self-flagellation is what it is," Merlin said one day but told me not to repeat it to anyone else.

On that particular occasion, Merlin blinked a little but stood his ground. "The Cherokees seem to like my new head piece," he said quietly. "I don't know that wearing a black hat and black suit is engraved on the missionary stone."

"Mister Montgomery, we've got souls to win and we've got to keep these Indians from descending into an everlasting hell. Now here you are dressing like them. The next thing I suppose you'll join them out at the ball play."

"That wouldn't be a bad idea," Merlin said. "Tell you what, sir, I'll make you an innocent wager. Let's give it a month, me wearing this turban. If we haven't baptized more Cherokees than the last month of my predecessor, then I'll take this turban off and throw it away."

Preacher Paul's fury seemed to die down a tad but his Adam's apple continued to quiver and was as red as a red delicious apple when he walked away.

As we rode north, the hours elapsed so quickly we found ourselves riding through a gap and looking down on a Cherokee village.

As we approached the cabin of a believer, youngsters came pouring out along with their small dogs. They ran alongside until we reached the clean swept front yard. The children who could speak English quickly greeted Merlin, being well-trained as to what to expect. "Hello, Missionary, remember me? I'm Red Bird." He was a little fellow with a sweet grin. "For God so loved the world, he gave his only begotten son.' John 3-16."

"Wonderful, Red Bird, come get your present."

Merlin swung down from his horse, opened his saddle-bag and pulled out a Y-shaped slingshot carved from sour-wood by some of his Cherokee friends. Red Bird looked at the slingshot with joy and volunteered to take the missionary's horse, give her some water and tie her to a tree.

I noticed a little girl on the outer fringe of the little crowd. She timidly approached Merlin with a great deal of hesitation. She caught Merlin's eye and spoke up:

"Missionary, here is my verse: 'Faith, hope and love. But the greatest of these is love.' —First Corinthians, chapter thirteen."

"Very good, young lady," Merlin declared, patting her on her head as he handed her a piece of homemade hard candy. "And what might be your name?"

"Running Deer, sir," she said, smiling timidly.

"You have not been to our school in Hi-wass'ee; where did you learn to speak English so well?"

"At Candy Creek Mission, sir, on the other side of the mountains in Tenn-a'see. But my family moved back here to be with my grandfather."

Running Deer's Indian mother spoke up to say that the little girl's grandfather was Cavenaugh Murphy, one of the area's old white traders.

"Mister Murphy," Running Deer said, "he is my grandfather. He lives alone. My grandmother pass on to Land Beyond. And Gran'pa is getting old and has a head of white hair."

"I would like to meet the gentleman," Merlin said, looking down at the little girl and her mother. "Could you take me to see Mister Murphy sometime?"

"Sir, I can take you there right now," Running Deer said. "He lives just through those trees on the other side of the branch."

Merlin remounted his horse and swung the girl up behind him. He put Alice into a slow trot and Running Deer grinned and held on tight around Merlin's waist. As I rode along behind, I could see the girl's long silky black hair waving behind her like a flag.

After fording the stream, we came up to Trader Murphy's cabin. It was perched on a gentle hill overlooking a yard of native grasses. The yard dropped off to a canebrake and a creek. From the wooded mountain behind the house, I could see the water running down the hillside. It obviously came from a spring near the hilltop, and I imagined it provided plenty of running water for Murphy's family, his livestock and his trading post customers. Hollowed out poplar troughs could be seen routing the water right by the cabin while one trough branched off to the barn lot.

Murphy's log cabin was surrounded with hardwood trees; a shady black walnut tree had a special place in front of his porch. His trading post was off to the side of his cabin. "Altogether a very agreeable situation," Murphy told us later.

As we came up, the old man was out on his front porch in his rocking chair, enjoying the sunshine and whittling away on a piece of wood.

Running Deer lost no time in scrambling down from the horse and racing to her grandfather, receiving a hug and a kiss. The old man looked up and said to us, "Mornin' men; light and look at her saddle."

Merlin swung down and one of the youngsters took Alice and ticd her to a post. Then he tied Bullet to a sapling.

"Hello, Mister Murphy," Merlin said. "I'm Merlin Montgomery, one of the missionaries to the Cherokees in the Hi-wass'ee Valley."

"I heard tell as much," the old man said. "Mighty proud to make your acquaintance."

"And this is my friend Little Jon Merion," Merlin said,

"who has taken a Cherokee name, Tsan-usdi."

"Glad to meet you, T'san," the old man said.

"Now Mister Missionary," he said. "What might be your reason in comin' to visit old man Murphy?"

"I was in the settlement and Running Deer told me about you, and I was curious to meet you."

"Glad to meet you both. Take a seat wherever you can find one."

Merlin sat down on the porch floor in front of the old man, with his feet down on a step, and I sat down on the steps next to Running Deer.

The old man pulled out his deep corncob pipe and stuffed it full of cured Indian tobacco. Running Deer raced to the fireplace inside and brought out a stick of fire, causing Murphy to grin with gratitude.

"Quite a grandchild you have there, Mister Murphy. She is becoming a Christian, you know."

"Oh?"

"Yes, sir. She gave me a Bible verse from one of Saint Paul's letters from his base at Ephesus on the Turkish coast, his letter to the Corinthians in Corinth, Greece."

"And what was that, pray tell?"

"Let Running Deer tell you."

"'Faith, hope and love,'" she said, "'but the greatest of these is love'—First Corinthians, thirteen-thirteen."

"Now exactly what does that mean, Mister Missionary?"

"Well, sir, Paul ended up as one of Christ's most devoted followers. That is after he was struck blind on the road to Damascus. Afterward, thanks to the Lord, he regained his sight and became what might be called a Christian radical, so great was his zeal and devotion to Jesus."

"Is that so?" Cavenaugh Murphy asked.

"Paul was telling us that as Christians we can have hope for this life and the one hereafter," Merlin said, "but that it takes a lot of faith and love for our fellow man. Such as the Lord's Second Commandment as recorded in the New Testament. Running Deer, can you repeat for us Christ's Second Commandment?"

"Yes, sir," she said. "Mark, twelve thirty-one: 'Thou shall love thy neighbor as thyself.'"

The missionary reached into his pocket and pulled out a little beaded necklace and presented it to Running Deer.

"Wal, Reverend, so that's one of your lord's major commandments, eh?"

"Yes, you might say that. Love is the central theme of being a Christian."

"Love? Are you joshing?"

"Not at all; do you find that strange? And by the way, just call me Merlin."

"Indeed I do find it strange, Merlin. If loving your neighbor is so important, why are you Christians, particularly your pious Philistines down in Georgee, so determined to beat their Cherokee neighbors out of their land? Not just their land, but their homeland, their very existence as a people. Those so-called Georgee Christians are doing their dead-level best to kick our Cherokees off their ancient territory in north Georgee; and north Al-a'ba'ma and even here in these Cherokee mountains."

Merlin squirmed a bit as the old man continued his angry rant.

"The Cherokees are the ancient owners of this country, Merlin, and they wish nothing other than to be left alone. Just why do they have to be moved to the west, anyway, beyond the Mississippi, and forced to leave behind the bones of their fathers?"

Merlin tried to avoid the old man's piercing blue eyes, turning his attention to Running Deer. After a pause, he turned back to respond.

"Well, sir, Trader Murphy, you have a very good point. We Christians have indeed fallen short of the mark. That's the way Paul would have put it. And I don't exclude myself. Right around here, for instance, we missionaries have failed to show real respect for the Cherokees, and their way of life. And I've been having problems with my church sponsors back in Charleston about this very question. Many of them support President Andrew Jackson's stated plans to force the red man out of this land that was given to them by God thousands of years ago."

"Moreover," Merlin continued, "I hear tell that most whites in Georgia and Tenn-a'see are downright unChristian in their attitude toward the Cherokees."

He added that, "We missionaries up here are doing our best to help our Cherokee friends in this time of turmoil."

"That's good to hear," Cavenaugh Murphy said.

Merlin then changed the subject: "Sir, I'm curious—how did you come to take up abode here in these Cherokee mountains?"

"This is the way it happened, Merlin. Years ago, my home was at Beaufort on the South Carolina coast. I had come there from Ireland. I first visited this country back in the seventeen hundreds, way before the big War of Independence. I made a lot of friends all through this Cherokee country and I learned the language. My business was dealing in furs, mostly deerskin. I bought the skins and hauled 'em to Charleston on my pack horses and sold them at a nice profit. Most of those pelts ended up in London. And to tell you the truth, when the Revolutionary War broke out in 1776, I sided with the British. I was what they called a Tory. Lot of my neighbors on the coast were, too.

"But the common folk, American patriots they called themselves, became numerous and soon took up arms against us Tories and the British troops coming in. When they started winning the war it became real dangerous for us Tories. I managed to make my escape early. Some of my Tory friends were not so swift and they died on the end of a rope."

Merlin and I were listening intently.

"It was only natural that I ended up here." he said. "The Cherokees were very kind to me, and allowed me to settle here in their country and even protected me.

"A few years after the war came to an end, I came out of hidin' and set up this tradin' post here. I took in a lot of furs and sold them to the younger traders from Charleston and brought back goods from down there for my store.

"'Course here in recent years, the fur business has jest about petered out. Our animal population has been declining, particularly the deer and the beaver."

The old man stroked his grizzly white beard and refilled his pipe. Running Deer dashed inside to bring out another piece of fire.

"After fleeing the Low Country and coming here, I found the Cherokees to be downright friendly and accommodatin'. A beautiful people, really. I married Ta-lu'la, the daughter of one of the head men, a sweet lady who bore me three wonderful children. My wife Ta-lu'la, bless her soul, passed on to her reward a few months ago. She lived to what we think was around seventy-three years of age. She was a wonderful helpmate; she taught me a lot about the Cherokee way of life and gave me love and affection and helped teach me their language.

"So for decades now," he continued, "I have been an adopted Cherokee. But now my days are numbered and I'm unable to get around much. I can still read, though. I get the Charleston paper from the pack horsemen. But I don't like much of what I'm readin'. The Cherokees have been forced to cede all of their land in South Carolina and most of their territory in Tenn-a'see and Kentuck. So all that's left is this little sliver of mountain land here in North Carolina and some tracts in Tenn-a'see and northwest Georgee where Cherokees migrated when brutally pushed out of their villages in the Lower Towns at the head of the Savannah River in South Carolina. And oh yes, the Cherokees still cling to little tracts of land along the Tenn-a'see River, and the Ku'sa Rivers in northeast Al-a'ba'ma and the northwest corner of Georgee."

Suddenly, the old man started talking about religion, and Merlin did not interfere.

"Merlin," he said, "I must tell you how proud I am of my granddaughter Running Deer who recited those Bible verses for you. God's a spirit, you know. Jesus came to our world as the Son of God in person and in spirit. Then, when he completed his work on earth He became a spirit and joined His Father in heaven.

"I get a chance every few months to go down to the Methodist camp meetin's. The Indians and the rest of us love to holler and whoop and sing at those gatherings, and sometimes I myself get to feeling the spirit of God. This thrill rises in my body, causin' me to feel like I can almost float in the air."

"Is that so?" Merlin asked.

"Yes, sir. Sometimes out there I get to feelin' like I'm in the middle of a bolt of lightnin', spinnin' around and around in a fiery glow. You know the Lord said in one place in the Bible—was it in Revelations and in Luke seventeen-twenty-four?—that in the last days, the Lord Jesus would return to the earth along with lightning flashin' from one end of the earth to the other. That's the way the end of the world will take place, like a giant bolt of lightnin' that'll wrap around the earth."

The old man snapped his finger. "Be just like that, in the twinkling of an eye."

Merlin was amazed at the old trader's recitation. "You're a wise man, Mister Murphy," Merlin said as he got up, "a very wise man. I'd like to come back and visit with you again sometime."

"Be pleased to have you come by anytime, brother Merlin, and you also, Jon-boy."

As we prepared to leave, I felt I had learned a lesson myself about the Spirit of God. And on our way back home the next day, I had a lot to think about and I couldn't wait to get back and relay my experiences to Gu'li. And I told Merlin that Gu'li and I need his advice in helping out our folks here in the valley, in case war should come to our end of the Cherokee Nation.

# CHAPTER EIGHTEEN

## Ma Takes Sick & Dies

A week before Christmas, Ma started coughing almost continuous through the night. And I noticed that her face had turned almost as white as cotton.

"I'll be all right, Jon-boy," she told me several times. "I'll be fit to be around in a few days." But then she started coughing again.

Instead of improving in the weeks to follow, she got worse, experiencing hacking coughs, chills and sweats. Also I could tell from her hands; they were still as beautiful as ever, especially her long fingers, but I noticed that blue veins were showing up dark on her white hands. I began to get awful worried and I told Merlin and Wa-gu'li that she was bad sick and getting worse. Su-ta'li was concerned also, and came up every day to look after Ma.

As she lay there between coughs, I had a strange deep-down feeling that maybe she didn't have much longer to live. It was about that time that Merlin came by and prayed with her. He put his left hand on Ma's head and with his right arm overhead, prayed to God that if He saw fit, to help her recover. Oak Tree told me the Indian priests were also asking their Creator God to give the Missionary Lady a new lease on life.

One night, Ma stared at me, intent like. It appeared to me that perhaps she was about to give up her fight to live. Or she may have felt that perhaps the Lord was calling her to heaven to be with Pa. Whatever it was, I felt the pull of the spirit that night. Ma suddenly looked so beautiful and peaceful; her blue eyes were sparkling bright and her streaked brown hair glistened. When I bent down near her, she pulled me on down and held me onto her breast for a long time and kissed me on the cheek and told me again how much she loved me. Naturally I had a hard time keeping from choking up; I couldn't help but shed some tears right then and there because I knew she was telling me goodbye.

Ma wanted to tell me again how I came to get my name.

"Son," she said, "do you recall how we chose your name?"

"I recollect some, Ma, but not too clear."

She motioned for me to pull up a chair.

"It was near Christmas. To make some money to tide us over a period of hardship, I agreed to look after the children of our neighbors, the Woertz family. Their mother had just passed away.

"I remember my first day there; I felt a little nauseous. The Woertz house had a strong smell to it and was filled with burning candles. They were a German Catholic family and I guess the odors came from their death rituals. In any event, every morning when I went back into their house, my stomach would start churning.

"One day, to liven things up, I decided to play a little game with the Woertz children, a game my sister and I used to play as kids. We called it, *Telling the Future*. We would close our eyes, take a Bible and open it up at random and run a finger down the page. Then we would open our eyes to read the verse under our fingers.

"The first time I did this, my fingers took me to Saint Luke, Chapter one, verse thirteen, where the angel appears and says, 'Fear not, Zechariah, for thy prayer is heard, and thy wife Elizabeth shall bear thee a son and thou shalt call his name John.'

"I thought to myself, this has nothing to do with me, and so I closed the Bible and closed my eyes again and flipped open the Bible a second time. To my amazement, when I opened my eyes, what was before me? The same page, same chapter and same verse.

"I continued to feel sick every morning about the time when I entered that house. So I decided to go to a doctor. After the examination, the doctor told me I was pregnant!"

Ma's face lit up when she told me that.

"The doctor told me I could expect my baby around

May. What a wonderful surprise! Then it dawned on me: That's what the Bible was telling me, Jon. I knew that the baby would be a boy and I knew what his name would be . . . Jon—you! And from that time onward, my friends never referred to the coming addition as anything other than Jon. And so, Jon-boy, you entered the world squalling, weighing eight pounds even. *So don't forget, Jon, that you were prophesied in the Bible! And you are truly a son of God."*

Well, I just sat there in wonder, not knowing what to say. It was the first time that the story of my early life on earth was told to me in such a clear way.

I kissed Ma goodnight and when I climbed the ladder up to my bunk in the loft, my heart was heavy and I stayed awake for long time, just lying there with my eyes open, thinking about my sweet ma and how much I loved her. I had a strong feeling that I was about to lose her, and that she was telling me goodbye.

Early the next morning, I went next door to see Talking Rock again.

"Ma's bad off," I told him. "She's so sick she won't even go outside any more to witness the sunsets."

Talking Rock walked back with me to the house, and went straight in to Ma's bedroom where she was lying in bed. When he came out, he was downcast. "You're right, Jon," he said, "Miz Rebecca is not well at all. I'm glad Su-ta'li comes to help her. But we need to get a doctor right away. I'll ask Spring Frog to ride down to the Presbyterian mission at Haweiss."

"Where's that?" I asked.

"It's way down on the Ku'sa River just beyond the Head of Ku'sa. They have a very good doctor down there who runs the Presbyterian mission—Michael McDougald. It'll take Spring Frog about a week to get there and back. And we can only pray that the good doctor will be able to come back with him and in time."

We were greatly pleased when Spring Frog came riding up to our cabin a week later, followed by the good Doctor McDougald on his big mare. Talking Rock took the doctor directly in to see Ma and it took him only a few minutes to figure out what was her problem. He came out and went into a huddle with our friends. I overheard him say that Ma had consumption, an ailment that affected the lungs.

"At this point," the doctor said, "there is precious little that can be done for her other than to urge that she stay in bed and get a lot of rest. Her illness appears to be at a fairly advanced stage. I will leave some luadenum here to relieve her pain, but I must tell you that she probably has no more than two months to live."

"Oh, Gracious Lord," Talking Rock said, totally shocked and seemingly at a loss as to what to do. Merlin said he'd pass on the latest word to the valley prayer chain, whose members had been praying for Ma for well over a week.

"To relieve Mistress Merion's coughing," the doctor said, "some of the local Cherokee medicine men might want to fix her a reduction of elm bark and boneset along with two teaspoons of root bitters."

The doctor was a kindly man, and he had a clipped brogue that Merlin said came straight out of Boston. He sat down on our porch and talked with Merlin and me.

"Jon," he said, "I hope you don't blame yourself for your mother's illness. There's nothing in the world that you could have done to prevent it that we know of. Other than to have gotten her to slow down a little, perhaps."

"Yes, she's been a busy worker," Merlin said after a long pause. "Every year, after the school summer school break, she traveled the valley constantly, helping Cherokee wives and children."

I couldn't help but partly blame myself for her ailment, particularly since she suffered so much on that frightful runaway wagon ride crossing the Un-i'coi Gap.

Gu'li came up and spent several days and nights with us, helping out in any way he could. He brought along several delicious dishes to our home, prepared by his mother, including persimmon pie.

A week later, Ma was gone. She died one night in her sleep. I walked into her bedroom to ask her what she wanted for breakfast. She was lying there white as a sheet with her hands crossed on her chest. I knew intuitively that she had died in her sleep. I held her wrist to check her pulse, but there was no pulse. I got down on my knees and laid my head on Ma's breast and cried for a few minutes. As I got up, I felt an ache in my heart and also relief, knowing that she was now in heaven and didn't have to suffer any more.

The funeral at the mission church drew a throng of Cherokees from up and down the valley, along with some neighboring whites and a few blacks, including, of course, our dear friends Isaac and Naomi, and, of course, members of the mission staff. I was pleased to see so many native flowers that had been made up into bouquets and hung all around the front end of the sanctuary and around the casket that had been hand made out of poplar wood by Oak Tree, Conrad and Hawkeye. Preacher Paul and Missionary Merlin gave beautiful eulogies and read some Bible passages that Ma always loved and the Cherokee choir sang so beautifully. The pall bearers were Oak Tree, Corn Silk and Fishing Hawk on one side, and Goliath Dan, Talking Rock and Merlin on the other side. Then, when they took her casket up to the burial ground near the top of a nearby knoll, several Cherokees came along carrying their own floral tributes and gently laid them all around the grave. When Hawkeye and his helpers heaped the last shovel of dirt to form the mound, the flowers and bouquets of green were spread over and around the grave.

The following day, in the late afternoon, Wa-gu'li, Merlin, Su-ta'li and Talking Rock joined me for a stroll up to the graveyard, arriving there at about sundown, Ma's favorite time. We looked at her grave as the sun was going down and thought about Ma and her life. I spent several minutes sobbing. "Why did it happen, and so quickly?" I asked.

"Jon, it was God's will is the only way I can explain it," Merlin said. "You can rest assured that your mother is a lot better off in heaven where she has joined your Pa."

"But why did she have to suffer so?"

"Jon-boy," Talking Rock said, "you're asking a question that we will have to ask God when we get to heaven. Just know that God will reveal himself in his good time. And just realize that your mother is now resting easy in heaven, along with your Pa. That's what I like to think about. You have wonderful memories of your mother and your father. Remember the sweet times."

We stood there, the five of us, in the evening stillness until the sun went down and the darkness came upon us.

# CHAPTER NINETEEN

## Where Shall I Live?

Right after Ma died and went to heaven, Goliath Dan and Kindness Haughton took me in, just like I was one of their own. I decided right off that I liked the arrangement, although Kindness could never in a million moons replace Ma in no way, shape or form. She was powerful sweet to me, though, and sure enough knew how to set a scrumptious table: sweet potato pones, fried sweet corn, field peas flavored with bear meat, and the most tasty cornbread that you've ever put in your mouth.

And all cooked right there in her fireplace using her crane pots, spiders and Dutch ovens. 'Course she roasted the sweet potatoes right there in the hot coals.

But even more than the good vittles was the joy of being around Dan and Kindness with all their carryings on. It was all new to me. My Pa, being a stern preacher man, didn't like much funning in our home in Virginia and frowned on us ever singing much. Ma went along with it although I had a feeling that she never did much like Pa's rules.

Now in Dan and Kindness's house, you never know what's going to happen next. He likes to pull out his old fiddle and play a tune on it, only he sits down and sticks the instrument on his left knee instead of under his chin. It's pure magic what comes out of that fiddle and it on his knee like that. Dan likes to invite a bunch of neighbor folks for a night of music-making and singing and dancing right there on their slick puncheon floor! And oh yes, Su-ta'li plays a Jew's harp and Hawkeye Hawkins a French harp and boy do we have fun, although all I can do is clap my hands and sing a little. Merlin's teaching me to play the mouth harp, what Ma used to call a harmonica.

The word around the valley was that Preacher Paul had got awful riled when he heard about Dan and Kindness's loud parties. Everyone was right relieved that he never brought it up in church.

But the best part in my new living arrangement is that Dan turns me loose of a day after school, permitting me to rove around as much as I wish. It's most always with my buddy Wa-gu'li, of course.

I felt awful obliged to Dan and Kindness for taking me in, being as I was an extra mouth for them to feed on top of their own twin young'uns. Plus their two hungry dogs.

"Ain't no more trouble to set five plates than four," Kindness said the day I arrived at their front door, which made me feel mighty welcome. "But you'll hav'ta act mighty pert at the table, Jonnie boy, do you want your share of the vittles!"

The day I arrived with my little leather bag of treasures, Goliath Dan was real nice to me, saying, "We're mighty proud to have ye in our home, boy." And after he told me I'd be sleeping up on the loft near the ladder, he declared, "Now T'san-usdi, we have only a few commandments around here. The main one is, you've always got to be home at Kindness's supper table by sundown unless ye got a durn good excuse." Which I agreed was right reasonable.

I had a fear deep down that this was just too good to last. And sure enough, the day came when Preacher Paul called me over to his office after school one day and told me that the church had to decide what they would do with me and that he was calling a church conference on the Saturday night before New Year's Day.

When Dan and Kindness and I arrived at the church house, Merlin and Hawkeye were already there, lighting the candles and placing them around the walls. The place looked right sparkly; I could still see green signs of Christmas all around—holly and rhododendron and cedar branches that the other lads and I had pulled in from the woods, plus here and there over the doors a few sprigs of mistletoe that Conrad Carreker had shot off of oak limbs with his long rifle. It pleasured Dan during the Christmas season to catch the womenfolk walking under the mistletoe so he could kiss 'em, and then laugh his big old belly laugh, causing the ladies to blush and run off screaming.

Preacher Paul had invited all the church members in good standing to attend—the missionary families, about a number of Cherokees including Su-ta'li, Corn Silk, Spring Frog, Oak Tree and Laugh-in'gal. There were a few white folks who were Bible-believing members and of course Jacob and Naomi, our black neighbors. Naturally Missionary Merlin was on hand, and oh yes, (how could I forget?), Wa-gu'li, who came in with his ma Su-ta'li, plus of course Talking Rock and Gilda Golden-feather.

After they sang "Amazing Grace," Preacher Paul walked up to the pulpit and said he'd called the church conference "to determine the future of our young orphan."

"*Orphan?*" I said to myself, "that's *me* he's talking about!" All the while, the preacher never did look down in my direction and I was sitting on the right hand front log betwixt Dan and Kindness. You would've thought he could at least have looked my way. Before going any further, Preacher Paul prayed a powerful prayer, calling on the Almighty for some special watching over on this night. Then he lit into the main subject:

"Brethren, with the death of Sister Rebecca, her son Jon is now left without a home, or a family."

Lord have mercy, this thing sounded serious. I got to

wondering to myself where I'd end up. The worst thing they could do would be to put me in with Preacher Paul and his wife. And I determined then and there if that happened, I would run away and take Gu'li with me if he'd go. If not, I'd set out on my own.

Preacher Paul walked back and forth across the front of the room, rubbing his long, bony fingers together in front of his chin like a church steeple. Then he'd stop and swing around to look out toward the back of the room, or the woods or somewhere else.

"Jon's uncle and aunt in Virginia have given us full authority to determine the boy's future," he said. "They wrote and said for us to do what was best in our eyes for the boy."

It was about then that I started looking around the room to see how many friendly faces I could see. I spotted Su-ta'li, Gu'li's ma. I had dreamed that just about the only thing better than being given to Goliath Dan's family would be to move in with Gu'li and Su-ta'li, but I knew chances of that ever happening were awful slim.

I knew the head missionary didn't like the way I was being raised by Dan and Kindness. Folks told me he had lined up the church conference to get me removed from their home. First one to speak up was the missionary farmer, Caleb Clark, who said his main concern was that I get a God-fearing raising and that he and his wife would volunteer to take me in.

*They what?* I started to jump up and holler, "*A thousand times no!*" I couldn't believe my ears. I didn't like Old Man Clark, anyway, nor his droopy wife, or their pitiful kids.

"Jon Merion is going to go the way of the pagan Indians and the devil if we don't stop him," Caleb Clark said. I could see he was right serious. He started chewing his tongue that was packed in his right jaw. Then Caleb Clark looked over and pointed his finger at me. "I see that boy everywhere running wild with his aboriginee friends. He needs to have the fear of God lashed into him before it's too late."

I knew what he meant by that. I'd heard his young'uns hollering at night and Gu'li said Caleb whipped them unmercifully with peachtree limbs, and for the tiniest of infractions.

I kept waiting for somebody to stand up and call for the church to do the right thing and give me a permanent home with Goliath Dan and Kindness. All my Cherokee friends seemed like they had been struck dumb, even Merlin. Preacher Paul must have surely put the fear of God in every last one of them.

"Well then," Preacher Paul said, "do I hear a motion that we turn the boy over to the Clarks?"

"So move," said Caleb Clark.

About that time, Comfort Carreker, the wife of the gentle German blacksmith who took Ma's place as a teacher at our school, raised her hand.

"Pastor Paul, may I speak?"

The head missionary nodded.

"Sir," she said, "everyone around the settlement knows that Jonnie is a right mischievous child."

I knew I was in for it now. Besides I thought I was a

young man, not a child. But there was more from Mistress Carreker:

"But what's wrong with a young boy who's filled with curiosity? At his age, Preacher Paul, you probably were the same."

Well, bless her heart, I was ready to stand up and shout *"Hallelujah! And Thank you, Mistress Carreker."* The head missionary turned a little red in the face and farmer Clark chewed on his tongue another time or two.

"True, he plays a lot with the Indian boy Wa-gu'li, Su-ta'li's son," Comfort Carreker said. "And being boys, they're well acquainted with all the woods and creeks around here. But Dan and Kindness are giving him a good home, a home with lots of love and affection. I think the Lord would be well pleased. I would be in favor of leaving him there. So I'd favor a motion along that line."

Well, you should've heard the commotion that comment aroused. The quiet Indians suddenly came alive, yelling and clapping their hands. Even old Oak Tree broke his usual silence and slapped his leg and grunted three loud grunts, real booming grunts. My buddy Wa-gu'li seemed to find his voice about then, and Corn Silk shouted out loud.

Caleb Clark jumped up and counter-attacked. He screamed that we couldn't allow the Devil to take me over, otherwise the whole lot of us were in trouble with the Lord and that the mission would burn in hell, along with the unsaved pagan Indians that he declared were in the worst fix of all.

Well, about that time, the new missionary, my friend

Merlin, stood up. I knew he was my friend because he allowed me to call him by his first name. On this night, Merlin had on Indian clothes: deerskin pants, moccasins and the like. I was a mite surprised when I saw he also had on an Indian bracelet and wore three feathers in his hair like the Cherokee men. I thought he looked pretty darn good.

"Reverend Paul, thinking seriously of this young man's future, shouldn't we get his opinion?" That was Merlin speaking.

"*HIS* opinion, Reverend Montgomery? You mean *the boy's opinion*? He's not of the age to have *an opinion*." That was Preacher Paul talking.

"Yes, Reverend Proctor, Jon's opinion and feelings should count. He's obviously an intelligent lad. I understand he's nearing fifteen-years-old. Let's ask him what he thinks we should do with him."

I couldn't believe he was talking' about me. Intelligent? That means smart, I thought. In any event, Comfort Carreker and my friend Merlin sure whipped up a hornet's nest there in that room. The Cherokees started whooping as only Indians can whoop and they began clapping again. I noticed Oak Tree whooped a little and that made me wonder: *Is that what a Indian war whoop sounds like?* Shrill and scary, *WOOOO-EEEE, WOOOO-EEEE, WOOOO-EEEE, WOOOO-EEEE!!!* Whatever it was, it seemed to put the Spirit of God in that room. Or maybe the Great Spirit Yowah. Or perhaps both.

Preacher Paul knocked his fist on the rostrum trying to get order and old man Clark started chewing his tongue again. I felt sorry for the both of them.

Finally Preacher Paul motioned for me to come up to the front and I edged up there. The crowd quieted down.

"Jon, how old are you?" Preacher Paul asked.

"Well sir, I was born on May tenth, eighteen ought eight. This being eighteen twenty-three, I guess that puts me at age fifteen."

"Reverend Merlin wants us to get your thoughts in this matter. Where would you like to live? Do you want go back to Virginia to live with your uncle and aunt? Or would you rather stay here in the valley?"

It was purely astonishing, the ignorance of Preacher Paul. 'Course it's hard to put much trust in a man who can't look at you straight in the eye when he's talking to you.

I caught sight of Merlin in the corner of my eye standing over on the other side of the room, and I thanked the Lord that he was on my side. Talking Rock and Gilda Golden-feather were there on the front log anxious bench acting right anxious and so was Su-ta'li and Oak Tree and Laugh-in'gal plus the Roartys, Rob and Rose. And naturally I thought about my buddy Wa-gu'li who was sitting on a log right up front with his ma. So I decided to speak:

"Sir, now that Ma and Pa are both gone, all of my friends in the world are right here in this valley, in this room, really," I said. "So if it was left to me, I'd just as soon stay put right here in this settlement."

"All right, then," Preacher Paul said. "Which brings us to the next question. Jon-boy, if you wish to live here, what do you think would be the best living arrangement for you?"

"Well, sir, if Mister Dan and his wife Kindness will keep me, I'd like to continue living right there with them, like I've been doing. I love them and they love me."

"Thank you, son," Preacher Paul said. "Does anyone else have any questions for Young Merion?"

Goliath Dan stood up: "Fellow Christians: Kindness and I are plumb pleased at the young feller's behavior since we took him in. 'Course sometimes he can get a mite contrary and rambunctious, being as he's got a strong will.

"As y'all know we don't believe in trying to break a child's will by beating 'em like some folks do. And yes, it's true, we don't have many rules at our house, 'cept we believe in one another. We get him to church on Sunday along with our young'uns and we insist on his school attendance. And we've got some chores that we demand of him around the house. We are right proud of Jon, who likes to be called by his Cherokee name, *T'san-usdi*. He helps out around the house and he minds me and Kindness. We'd shorely like to keep him if the church members see fit."

The whole church full of people roared their approval and went into another noisy applause. Well, that just about did it. Preacher Paul could see that he was outnumbered, and he called for a new motion. Merlin got up and said, "I move that we put Jon Merion in the permanent protection of Dan and Kindness Haughton."

"Second the motion," Mister Carreker yelled. On a show of hands, the yeas had it almost unanimous and the Cherokees whooped and hollered some more. Caleb Clark stomped out, fuming. Talking Rock grabbed me up and swung me around and Merlin came up and shook my hand with a big handshake like I was a man. I almost cried when Gu'li near bout kissed me, with a big bear hug and Su-ta'li picked me up and did just that, kissing me right smack on my right cheek! I felt so deliriously happy that I would stay in friendly hands and could keep my freedom, I could hardly think. I knew that now I'd have to do my dead level best to live up to Dan's confidence in me. Plus that of Kindness, of course, along with the whole church full of sweet folks.

My only regret was that Ma and Pa weren't there to see what had happened to their little runt of a boy. 'Course I knew they were looking down with smiles from heaven and were able to see the whole thing for themselves. I prayed a silent prayer thanking the Good Lord above.

# CHAPTER TWENTY

## Spying on the Priests

By the time the first full moon of the following Spring rose over the valley, Wa-gu'li and I had just about become twins, excepting he had black hair and I had red hair. And of course he had brown eyes and I had blue eyes. You couldn't ask for more powerful examples of red and black and brown and blue.

One afternoon I heard the whippoorwill whistle and I knew right off that Gu'li was nearby, heading to our secret place. I raced down the path by the cornfield, then galloped like a stallion by the canebrake and to our hideout. I tore open the vine door and wiggled in on my belly like a snake.

Gu'li was already inside and was in our small swimming hole. I stripped down, climbed up on our big rock, pinched my nose and jumped into the deep hole feet first. I purely enjoyed rising back to the top, holding my breath all the way.

Gu'li belly-busted several times, and the noise caused me to worry if the loud sounds we were making might give away our secret location.

And before the day was done, I learned to swim on my back, thanks to Gu'li. I surprised myself at how easy it was. 'Course Ma always said that as a little kid I took to water like a fish. We swam and dived most of the afternoon 'til we were plum give out, then we talked a long spell, mostly about spirits, his kind and my kind, and about Cherokee priests and conjurers. I learned that the keys to the Cherokee religion were fire and water.

"The Great Spirit is everywhere, T'san," Wa-gu'li told me, sort of repeating what he had related to me before. "We worship every living thing that springs from the Creator's hand—the rivers and the trees and the animals. But the greatest of all are the living fire and the living water."

Well sir, I knew that water and fire were important to the Cherokees, but Gu'li put it on an even higher standing. "The fires that burn in our council houses were handed down to us by the Great Spirit thousands of winters ago," he said. "We use them to rekindle fires when we clean out our cabins after burning all the past year's trash. At the same time, we ask forgiveness for all of the bad things that we've said and done to our brothers and even our enemies during the past year. Even bad thoughts."

"Goodness gracious, Gu'li," I said, "You folks are a lot more strict than we are in celebrating the start of a new year. About all most of us did on New Year's Day up in Virginia was to set off firecrackers, and a few people wrote down resolutions."

Gu'li elaborated further: "At the beginning of our new year—what the Una'kas call the spring—when life is springing back in the fields and forests, our Cherokee fire-keepers put new fires in our fireplaces, using the flames from the town house.

"The fire burns forever at every town house, just as the Great Spirit goes on forever. Each family gets a piece of new fire to start the new flame in their cabin. That gives our homes and villages a new life, and it gives a new life to every person in each house—a completely new start."

"What a wonderful tradition, Gu'li," I said. He told me that Cherokee families also "go to the water" at least once a year to get purified, "and at other times when we want to get right with the Great Spirit. Of course the priests go to the water for renewal at sunrise every day as do many of the older heads."

Gu'li promised to take me to the river the next time there was a purification rite. "Our number one *Ad-hon'ski* for A-quo'hee is A-sa'la Car-tee'kee, the Priest of Fire," he said.

"Yes, I remember him," I said. "He's the one who walked out on the mill house dam during that terrible storm and prayed to the Great Spirit to stop it. The rest of us were praying to our God for the same thing, but Oak Tree and other Cherokees felt that A-sa'la was really the one whose prayer convinced the Great Spirit to intervene."

"Oak Tree told me about that," Gu'li said. "And, by the way, Oak says A'sa-la is having a fire dance and Big Talk tonight. All the conjurer priests from A-quo'hee will be going. Why don't we go spy on them?"

"*Spy on them?*" I asked, with a big question mark in my voice. "That'd be a mighty dangerous thing to do, wouldn't it?"

"It would be if they was to catch us, but I won't let that happen. I'm sure we can slip up and look on from a distance without being seen."

Before the day was over, we had made our plans to go spying on the priests in the deepest dark of the night. And I thought to myself that this may help us identify some of the conjurer priests who lately have been causing some devilment against the missionaries.

It was way past our going-to-bed time when I slipped out of my corner of Goliath Dan's loft. Earlier in the day, Dan had given me permission to join Gu'li on the trip. "But be careful," he said, "and get back as soon as you can."

The twins were sleeping on their bunks downstairs; they had gone out like a light the minute they piled into their beds after dark. Goliath Dan was a sound sleeper, too, and his snore sounded like he was cutting logs with a crosscut saw.

Instead of going down the ladder, I slid silently on the slick sourwood pole. Just as I tiptoed to the door, I heard Kindness gulping, catching her breath. I froze in my tracks, and then I heard her starting up a light snore again and I headed for the door. I was barefoot, carrying my moccasins in my left hand.

I gently lifted the latch and slipped out, quietly returning the wooden door to its rightful place. I realized it was a little dangerous, but I figured I wouldn't be gone long. As I left the house I left the latch string out, and I quieted Dan's dogs with some biscuits. They crawled back under the house without barking.

As I walked down the path in my moccasins, I looked up into the sky and noticed low-flying clouds blowing across. Every little while, the moonlight filtered through the trees. I dared not light a torch, but I picked up a chunk of litard wood and took it along just in case we'd need it.

When I got farther along, I stuck two fingers in my mouth and, quiet like, issued my whistle. Straight away, Wa-gu'li whistled his reply. I hurried on.

As I was trotting along, Gu'li—trying to have some fun—came up behind me in the forest and grabbed me around the ribs. I jumped like a jack rabbit, being so shocked, and I almost fainted from pure fright. I flopped down on the ground to catch my breath.

Finally, I got back to breathing natural and Wa-gu'li asked me if I was ready to head out. "I'm about ready," I replied, "but please don't ever do that to me again. I know you're awfully good, like all Indians are, at moving through the woods so quiet like.

"By the way," I added, "I have a stick of litard for a torch if we need it."

"Good. But let's not use it now, T'san. On nights like this when the moon's fairly strong, we Cherokees depend on our eyes alone. The night varmints do it all the time and some of our sharp-eyed people can see by the light of fireflies, if there's enough of 'em."

All the priests had already gone to the site during the afternoon, so we felt confident that the trail alongside Persimmon Creek would be free of foot traffic. Even so, wearing our moccasins, we practiced walking quietly, without making a sound, and avoided stepping on a dead twig or small limb.

We kept moving deeper into the forest and came up to a small creek that we had to ford. The water was swift and cold, but we managed to cross it quickly by walking across the flat rock. Then we came onto the trail that would take us to the meeting site.

"You certain the priests are holding their talk tonight, Gu'li?"

"Positive. Runners came through yesterday and told Oak Tree the meeting would occur past midnight. Most of the honored men and conjurer priests started out earlier today."

Gu'li stopped suddenly. "What's the matter?" I asked.

"Be quiet," he whispered. "I hear something."

We stood like statues for such a long time I thought I'd topple over. Gu'li was holding his head high with his ear cocked.

"Hear that?" he whispered.

"Yes, it's a faint boom, boom, boom. A drum?"

"Yes. That's announcing the soon start of the talk. It's not too far now, maybe a mile through that gap ahead. Let's hurry! " We were moving along now by the light of the moon.

We started walking faster and, every so often, broke into a trot. We didn't want to miss a thing. I could hear the drumbeat echoing from the valley ahead. Nearing the crest of the hill, we slowed down to a slow walk. When we came around a bluff, we saw the conjurer crowd all spread out down below us in the bottoms, a circle of folks in strange animal masks and many carrying torches. We found us a nice spot behind a big oak tree to watch from. There was plenty of undergrowth to hide behind.

"Lord have mercy!" I whispered, after seeing what looked like three black bears to one side. I quickly realized they were Cherokees in bear skins. Gu'li said that yes, that's what they were. A big bonfire was burning in the middle of the field and it gave off speckled shadows through the meadow and trees. My nose picked up the fragrance of pine needles burning in the fire. I shivered just contemplating the scene.

For a good while, Gu'li and I just stood there on the hillside, watching. Finally, he came up to my ear and whispered: "See over on the other side next to the willow trees? Those are the medicine men and lower conjurers, sitting on big bear skins. And that's A-sa'la there in the middle, the head priest, in his costume."

"A-sa'la?"

"Yes, T'san. Can't you tell? He's the one with all the eagle feathers on his cape. They came from eagles he shot himself."

"Amazing! "

We slipped over to the lip of the hill and lay down near a bunch of laurels and then I saw the Priest of Fire clearly, he of the *Ad-hon'ski*, A-quo'hee's high temple of conjurer priests. In addition to his shiny cape of eagle feathers, his face was painted up in white and red.

I could see what Wa-gu'li meant when he mentioned A-sa'la as being seven score winters of age. His hair had turned a bright silver that seemed to reflect the light of the torches. Even his hair contained two eagle feathers. And when he strode across to the fire, his walk was slow and dignified, a walk that was different from everybody else's.

The lesser priests followed in circling the fire while the drums beat madly. There must have been a dozen of the conjurers, all wearing bright capes. Then coming behind were more Cherokees in regular get up, village head men, called chiefs by many whites. On the outside circle there came more men in animal skins and masks, some of them wearing deer heads and, of course many bear look-alikes.

What a sight!

The drums went silent and the crowd moved back from the fire and got ready for the talk. The Priest of Fire raised his arms, showing off his eagle feathers in all their glory. The outside ring of folks got down on their right knees. Then the Priest of Fire lowered his arms and started to speak.

His deep voice boomed across the valley. I couldn't understand a word at first, but Gu'li told me what he was talking about—that this was one of the Cherokees' long held traditions—The Fire Dance—and that the Una'ka whites must never take it away from them. Then he went on to say that some of the white missionaries were trying to kill their traditional events such as their nighttime dances, their ball play and even the Green Corn festivals.

"We Cherokees are going to have to recapture our old ways before they all disappear," A-sa'la said. "Besides that, the Georgia politicians in Milledgeville are scheming to take away our homeland. They want to send our people to the west, beyond the mother of rivers. Even those of us up here in these mountains outside of Georgia's borders."

A-sa'la Car-tee'kee was growing angry. "Way back, in far olden times," he told the crowd, "the Great Creator

God put our Cherokee ancestors down into this enchant-
ed land, to remain forever. But today our tribe is in danger
of losing it all. The whites want to take our sacred homeland, our rivers and mountains, even the hillsides where
the bones of our fathers lie."

"What does it mean, Gu'li?" I said, as we sat there under
the tree.

"It might mean war, T'san. It could come to that if the
Una'ka leaders from Georgee send in troops to try to run
us out."

We looked back down to hear A-sa'la continuing his ti-
rade, criticizing the missionaries for attempting to squelch
their ancient traditions. "It's devious and deceitful what the
missionaries are doing," A-sa'la said, "especially Preacher
Paul. He talks about saving our souls but he acts like he's
trying to clean our Cherokee souls from our bodies. We do
not have Una'ka souls and we never will."

Hearing all that talk, and even though the dancing had
not started, Gu'li and I got a little fearful and decided we'd
better head back home. We were afraid that if we stayed
much longer, we might get caught. Then Goliath Dan and
Talking Rock would clamp down on us bad. So while the
fire dancing got started, we hurried back down the trail.

I reached our cabin without incident, well before dawn,
and I was mighty glad that Dan was a deep sleeper. I gave
the dogs my last biscuits, and I said a silent prayer of thanks

to the Lord that our little adventure had gone off without any problem. "Thanks to God's angels," I said to myself.

As I quietly slid onto my pallet on my back, I prayed for the future of our nation. And then I got to thinking about what the Priest of Fire had said, but I didn't ponder long. Sleep comes awful easy when a body's tired. I remembered back to the time when I was a little lad. Ma and I were sitting on our porch steps in Virginia after she'd had a hard day working in the fields.

"La, I'm tired," I remember Ma saying.

"Me tired, too, Mama," I replied.

That was the kind of night it was. Soon my weary bones entered the never never land of sweet sleep. I remember my last thought: Maybe we should go on another spying trip soon. I hoped so.

# CHAPTER TWENTY-ONE

### Meeting the Priest of Fire

I roused out early the next morning and splashed cold water on my face from the wooden bucket on the back porch. It would be a bright summer day and I felt good being alive and living with Goliath Dan and Kindness and getting to know Missionary Merlin real well and, of course, many of the Cherokees and whites and blacks in the valley.

I was beginning to fall in love with all of 'em, in particular Wa-gu'li, Talking Rock, and Oak Tree and maybe even the *Ad-hon'ski* priests. But I wanted to learn more about A-sa'la Car-tee'kee, the Priest of Fire, the one we had spied on.

I figured the best way to start off was to visit Talking Rock early in the morning while he was still at home. I determined for once to hog-tie my flutter-mill—my loose tongue—especially about our recent spying activities. I had a feeling that he probably suspicioned that we'd been up to some sort of devilment like that. Deep down I had a feeling also that he would have loved the way we carried out our spying, thanks to God's angels who had been protecting us.

When Gilda Golden-feather invited me in, Talking Rock was already at the table. "Hey boy, what you doing up so early?" he asked as I walked in. "You up to something nefarious?"

He kept grinning at me as I pulled up my chair. Gilda was getting hoe-cakes from a spider skillet along with a pile of venison bacon from another skillet. The smell was heavenly. She put down mugs of hot coffee before us and I breathed the aroma in deep. It felt wonderful being there where God's sweet smells seemed to congregate, along with friendly talk.

"Watch out, fellers," Gilda yelled, "these hoe-cakes are coming up scorching hot!" Also in front of us on the table was a gourd full of wild sourwood honey plus a platter of of fresh butter churned by the young scholars. It was an early morning feast.

Talking Rock lowered his head and mumbled the blessing in his nonstop monotone: "Lord, make-us-truly-thankful-for-these-and-all-other-blessings-Amen." And just about as fast, we tore into our hoe cakes.

After I'd taken a few bites and downed a good gulp of coffee, since I had graduated to drinking coffee "straight" at times like this, I asked Talking Rock, "What do you know about A-sa'la Car-tee'kee, the Priest of Fire?"

"Ah ha! " he said, holding his fork in mid air. "So *that's* what's on your mind! A-sa'la! Well, I'll tell you one thing, T'san, he's a right powerful Cherokee holy man in these parts. And he comes from a long line of priests and conjurers, legendary spiritual leaders amongst the Cherokees."

"He sure is that, Jon-boy," Gilda joined in, returning to my old name, "A-sa'la Car-tee'kee's ancestors kept up the spirits of Cherokees hundreds of winters ago, when the situation in our nation had turned grim."

"When was that?"

"Mostly back in the seventeen hundreds from what I've heard," the chief said. "It's a miracle our people didn't disappear from this end of North America. The *Ad-hon'ski* were the only hope we had. They rallied our people up from near total despair."

"I had no idea it was that bad," I said.

"Those were bad times, T'san. To begin with, the early Europeans brought in smallpox they'd picked up from the slave ships and half of the nation's population died terrible deaths in the epidemic that followed. Many survivors committed suicide when they saw their scarred faces in the first mirrors brought in by the traders."

Gilda poured us more coffee and came and sat down with us. "Get you some more hoe-cakes and honey, T'san!" she urged. "Don't be bashful."

"Then in 1761," Talking Rock continued, "the British governor at Charles-Town sent in a thousand-man army of bayoneted white rifles to the Cherokee Lower Towns, terrorizing the people and destroying their little cabins and even their fields of corn."

He told me the story about one of the British army's lieutenants, Francis Marion, who was filled with anger and sadness when forced to burn down the pitiful Indian cabins around Keowee at the headwaters of the Savannah River.

Talking Rock pulled out a document brown with age and frayed on the edges. It quoted Marion—who later became the Revolutionary War's Swamp Fox hero fighting the British Redcoats in the Carolina Low Country—as coming to near tears after being forced to burn down the small Cherokee cabins, then being ordered to take their bayonets and slash down the young stalks of corn, the Indians' main sustenance. Most survivors, including children, fled in terror into Georgia. Then later, the cruel Britishers carried their reign of terror on up to the Middle Towns and in the Overhill Towns in East Tenn-a'see.

"During all those tragic years," Talking Rock said, putting down the paper, "my Cherokee grandmother told me our priests held our people together as well as they could, giving hope for the future."

"I don't see how it could have gotten worse," I said.

"Well it did. Leading up to the American Revolution on the seventeen-seventies," Talking Rock said, "white riflemen began pouring into our nation from Virginia and Tenna'see, killing innocent women and children all around this area and in East Tenn-a'see because the Cherokee Na-tional Council elected to send our warriors to support the British Crown during that big war."

Talking Rock poured himself another cup of coffee. "In recent years, Gilda and I have become born-again Chris-tians. But we understand how Cherokees, and full-bloods in particular, stand by their priests along with the old tra-ditions."

For several days I pondered what they had told me that morning, and my heart grieved even more for the poor Cherokees and their sad history. That made me want more than ever to learn more about the *Ad-hon'ski* priests.

That afternoon, Gu'li met me at our secret place and we talked about our recent spying adventure and recalled the power of the Priest of Fire in stopping the awful thunder-storm, or so most Cherokees believed.

"Do you think the Priest of Fire really possesses the power to do something like that, to stop the rain?" I asked.

"Possibly," Gu'li said. "One time I saw him call for rain during a long dry spell. A day later, showers came and the whole settlement joined in a big frolic outside in the downpour."

"Really?"

"Yes indeed. Now if you really want to learn about the Priest of Fire, T'san, you need to go watch him perform one of his daily rituals. It will be easy to go spy on him."

Being one to never turn down a dare, and with school being out during the harvest season, I agreed to go with Gu'li early the following day down to A-sa'la's cabin.

I revealed our plan to Goliath Dan and he reluctantly gave me permission to join Gu'li on the mission. "But be careful, boy," he said. "We don't want to stir up the conjurer priests."

So right before the crack of dawn the following Saturday, we headed south to the priest's home across from the River Hi-wass'ee.

By now I had become almost as clever at slipping through the woods quietly like a ghostly phantom as Gu'li, and Goliath Dan congratulated me on my quiet ways in the woods.

We reached our spying base on a hill near A-sa'la's cabin and got us a good location with a good view but we hunkered down behind a bank of blooming rhododendrons as our main cover.

"A-sa'la generally comes down to the river right after the sun rises over the trees," Gu'li said. "He'll probably be wearing only his dark blue loin cloth and a light calico shawl."

Just as I stuck my head up, there he was, as bright as day, right square in front of us as he walked out of his cabin. "I see him" I said, in a loud whisper.

"*That's him,*" Gu'li whispered.

Slyly, I peeked through the rhododendron leaves again and saw him walking slowly down to the river. He had on the loin cloth but he wasn't wearing his turban this morning. I could see that his hair gleamed like a silver ball as we had seen him a few nights before. As he approached the river, I could see that he was tall and elegant and was walking softly in his moccasins. I wasn't close enough to tell the color of his eyes but I could see he had a faraway look toward the bright sun that was rising over the tree tops.

A-sa'la paused to look down into the quietly swirling waters. Then he sang out a chant and kept it up for a good while. His voice had a mournful sound and I shivered with joy just listening. Then he began chanting again along with a prayer.

Although I'd become pretty good at understanding the Cherokee language, I asked Gu'li to link it for me so I'd not miss anything and it went like this:

> *Great Spirit of the River:*
> *I can feel that you are angry.*
> *I saw your brother the lightning*
> *last night, followed by the spirit thunder,*
> *trying to get our attention, to tell us something.*
> *I feel that you are speaking out*
> *against the white missionaries*
> *who are corrupting our people with new ways.*
> *And Great Spirit, thank you again for stopping the rain,*
> *which I requested as a favor*
> *to the plea of my brother, Oak Tree*

A-sa'la laid aside his moccasins and walked out into the river and edged into the deep part of the river. I could see that he seemed to have a powerful yet serene look.

All at once, I felt a surge that seemed to pierce my body like a bunch of needles, reminding me of the night the lightning struck the mill house. At the same time, I noticed the head priest was staring straight toward us, and he didn't shift his gaze!

"Who is up there, behind that bush?" he called out in Cherokee.

"He's seen us!" Gu'li whispered. "I felt a jolt hit me just as his eyes looked this way."

"Come down here and make yourself known," the priest said. "I don't see you, but I feel you. There are two of you. Walk down here immediately."

"Let's run, Gu'li."

"No, T'san, we'd better do as he says. It doesn't pay to disobey a conjurer priest." Gu'li rose up and started down the hillside and I followed along. A-sa'la motioned for us to join him in the water. We approached him, walking slowly out to knee-deep water.

"Well, who do we have here?" the priest asked in Cherokee. "Seems I should know you," looking at Gu'li.

"I am Little Fox, son of *A'huh-lee'hee* Jim Eagle, who died at the To-ho'pe'ka battle in A-la'bam'a. Some people call me Wa-gu'li because I can whistle like a whippoorwill."

"Is that so?" A-sa'la said, raising his eyebrows.

I was amazed at the priest's friendly yet strong looking face. Yet he had a holy presence about him. I couldn't believe this was the same man who spoke so strongly against the missionaries at the Ad-hon'ski gathering.

"Let me hear you whistle like a whippoorwill, Wa-gu'li," the priest requested.

Wa-gu'li stuck two fingers in his mouth, took a deep breath and issued a sharp whippoorwill call, then followed with a second. The whistles echoed through the valley. I saw some birds whirling back our way, looking to see where the call came from.

"I can see why your friends call you Wa-gu'li," the priest said. "You whistle well, young one, just like a whippoor-will."

A-sa'la turned his gaze onto me, but he kept talking to Gu'li.

"And who is your paleface friend here?"

"We call him T'san-us'di, Little Jon. His name, sir, is Jon Merion, the missionary orphan boy. His parents have passed away and he lives with Goliath Dan and Kindness Haughton. Dan runs the missionary grist mill along with Oak Tree."

"Ah, yes," the priest said, patting me on the head. "Talking Rock and Oak Tree have spoken of you, T'san."

I nodded and smiled at him. He smiled back. His eyes reminded me of sorghum syrup. They were so brown and bright and he seemed to be looking straight through me.

"Now tell me, Wa-gu'li," A-sa'la said with a jovial grunt, "why were you two up there in hiding, watching me?"

"Just curious, sir. T'san has been asking about you. He wants to know more about you, so I brought him to get a close look."

"Why didn't you come to my cabin and ask to see me

there?"

"We were afraid, sir."

"All right, young ones, here is what we will do. I wish for you both to join me for my next class of young braves at my asi hot house four moons from now. We will have a talk."

The head priest let us go and told us he wouldn't reveal to anyone about our spying on him, but that we needed to let our folks know about the upcoming hot house visit.

As we left, I told Gu'li that getting to meet the Priest of Fire like that was a godsend.

"But I'm a little fearful of going to his hot house meeting," I said.

"No need to worry, T'san, It will be a lot of fun."

# CHAPTER TWENTY-TWO

## A Town House Burns

We were having a severe late summer heat wave and Wa-gu'li said only a good soaking rain could break the back of the hot weather.

I felt sorry for the older scholars who had the task of cutting down the high standing rows of sorghum cane. Caleb Clark, a helper at the farm, said that their working in the hot midday sun would develop their character. "Sweat's good for a body," he said.

On the other hand, I noticed that most Cherokees dearly loved to retreat to their cool forests during the noon-time heat. "The Great Spirit doesn't intend for people to suffer so," Gu'li told me. "That's why he has provided us with the shady glens and cool springs and streams."

But in the waning days of our pale face August, we almost forgot about the weather when an uproar arose among the full-bloods and their priests. It began one night, just past midnight, when loud drumbeats woke me up, and Kindness and Dan too.

"Sounds like they're coming from the other side of the creek," Dan said. The following night, the booming drum beats started up again, and even louder. Angry drumbeats they were, fast and furious, and they continued for several nights, with the echoes riding the winds down through the valley.

"What do you think it means, Dan?"

"I'm puzzled, to tell you the truth," he said. "Those drums sound awfully scary. Why don't you ask Gu'li?"

"I plan to do that," I said. "Maybe it has to do with the protests the conjurers are raising," I said.

"Protesting what, Jon-boy?" Kindness asked, using my old name.

"I hear they're upset because Preacher Paul and Missionary Merlin have been violating their holy rivers with more baptisms here lately. You know the missionaries use the very same pools in Persimmon Creek and the River Hi-wass'ee where the priests and other full-bloods go to cleanse their souls of a morning."

"I wish Talking Rock was around so we could get him to sit down and talk to the full-bloods and find out what this is all about," Dan said. "But he's way off in Augusta for a while yet."

I went over to Wa-gu'li's the next morning. He agreed something was happening among the full-bloods. "There's a lot of ugly talk going on," he said, "and people are fiery mad. Not only amongst the priests and full-bloods, but also the ordinary Indians in their clans. We can only hope they don't turn to violence."

"Like using guns?" I said. "Heaven forbid. 'Course all the Cherokees I know are peaceable and easy going, headed by you and Corn Silk and Su-ta'li, Oak Tree and Laugh'in-gal, of course, and Talking Rock and Gilda Golden-feather."

"Take Oak Tree," I said. "I consider him as being almost saintly; he walks around with such serene dignity, and is as kind, dependable, and as strong as the tree he is named for."

"Unfortunately, T'san, you're quite ignorant about the feelings of the older heads, particularly the full-bloods. Many feel they're not being respected by the missionaries. There's a growing resentment boiling up amongst them."

"Why is that?" I wanted to know.

"The latest fury came when Preacher Paul came up with some new rules," Wa-gu'li said. "He posted some talking leaves saying the church will not countenance future heathen festivals, frolic dances and ball plays. And he told some of his church members he would oust any member who calls on conjurers for medication or seeks divine intervention by a heathen god."

"Oh my Lord, Gu'li," I said, "No wonder they are angry. I would be too if I was in their moccasins."

The following Sunday, I could see the resentment on the faces of the older Cherokees attending the worship service as the word got linkstered to those who were unable to read the talking leaves. Even the younger set who could read the decree were resentful. Eyes that had been merry before had narrowed into hardness.

"They're upset that the missionaries are trying to replace their ancient traditions with strict rules," Gu'li said. "Like Chief Tuck-a'lee-chee. He'd have to do away with one of his two wives."

"He has two wives?"

"For true, T'san. It is a long tradition that is allowed in the Cherokee Nation," he said.

"Who is he married to?"

"Two cousins. Married them both in a single Cherokee wedding."

"Married to two cousins? Do they stay in the same cabin?"

"Of course not!" Gu'li said. "He has two cabins and two families. Of course the wives, being cousins, visit back and forth all the time. They get along just fine."

"How many children are there?" I asked.

Before Gu'li could tell me more, a runner rushed up.

"*FIRE! Eu-har'lee Town House!*" the runner said, breathing hard. "*Big fire before sunup.*"

As soon as the runner got his breath, he left on the trail going north.

Gu'li and I took off running down the path that took us to Eu-har'lee, two miles down Persimmon Creek. Su-ta'li ran with us, too, but fell behind, being unable to keep up with our young legs.

It was a pitiful sight. The old Town House had gone up in smoke. A pile of smoldering ashes was most all that was left. Wisps of smoke hung like a little fog over the scene.

There was a huge hole in the ground. I figured that was where the old circular underground meeting room was located. We could see the rows for seats that had been carved from the earth. Gu'li pointed to the far end of the pit where the village's eternal flame had been burning over the years.

"That's where the chief and council members sat for meetings, around the sacred fire," he said.

Although I'd never been inside, I tried to remember what the Council House had looked like from the outside…a seven-sided building of vertical poles with a roof of poles and bark.

Well sir, I felt heartbroken for the Indians who were milling around, looking over the sad scene, seeing only a pile of ashes where the proud building once stood. The heart of the village had been destroyed, had gone up in smoke.

The crowd continued to grow. Many were in tears, especially the women. And I could hear sad grunts from the men.

Gu'li and I walked over to the far edge, where we saw the village chief, *Ta-wa'di* The Hawk, walking slowly around the ring of ashes, as if mourning for the dead. His craggy face with his hook nose and pockmarked cheeks appeared to show more hurt than anger.

Talking Rock showed up about then, just back from Augusta. The people opened up a path for him to reach *Ta-wa'di*. We edged up closer so we could hear. They talked in Cherokee. I could tell some of what was said but Wa-gu'li linkstered so I could understand everything.

"How'd it happen, Ta-wa'di?" Talking Rock asked. "Was it *ana-ga-liski* (a lightning strike)?"

"No *ana-ga-liski*," the chief said as his mouth turned tight and straight. *Ta-wa'di's* forehead was creased with worry wrinkles.

"Was lighted by some one," the chief added, looking up from the desolation.

"How do you know?" Talking Rock asked.

"No *ana-ga-liski* marks left on trees," the chief said. "And no boom. I would have heard *aya'da-qua'lo* (thunder) if lightning had hit here."

"So you're certain it was set?"

"Without doubt. Look at path of wheat straw coming from the north."

There it was, as plain as day. A line of wheat chaff had fallen on the trail leading up to the Town House.

The head man's guards kept curious moccasins from crossing the line. Then some of the young braves brought up pine saplings and set up a fence on both sides of the wheat chaff line, to protect the evidence.

"That's awful strong sign," Talking Rock told Ta-wa'di. "Only the mission farm would have wheat straw like this. You think someone from the farm did it?"

"Yes," he said, his face still holding its sad countenance. Talking Rock's eyes blazed with anger. "It's hard to believe that someone could be so lowdown. But the sign is there for all to see."

A long pause of silence ensued. The throng had grown quiet. Then Talking Rock spoke up. "*Ta-wa'di*, I'm going to do some checking on this. I'll be back."

He left quickly and we decided to follow him. We noticed he was holding his head down as he walked, following the line of wheat chaff. Just down the way, he suddenly stopped at a wide place on the trail. We stopped and jumped into the bushes because he was circling around, examining the ground on both sides of the trail. Then he resumed his walking.

After he had gone ahead, Gu'li and I went straight to where Talking Rock had stopped. The marks on the ground were clear. A sled had been there. The hoof marks of a horse were there, also. "That's how they brought the wheat straw from the mission farm stable, T'san," Gu'li whispered to me.

When we looked up, Talking Rock was headed toward the mission barn. So we started out in a trot. Thank goodness we had on moccasins. We were as quiet as Indian scouts as we watched him go into the barn yard and the stables.

"He's looking for more sign," Gu'li said.

We didn't have to wait long. Talking Rock came storming out of the barn and headed up the hill in the direction of the main mission buildings. After he got a distance away, we dashed over and ran into the barn. There we found a big pile of wheat straw, ready for use in the stables. We could see sled marks that came right to the stable. Apparently that's what Talking Rock saw, too.

We waited inside the barn to give Talking Rock time to get up to the mission compound. We knew he'd be heading straight to Preacher Paul's cabin.

When we saw him going around the corner to the other side of the head missionary's home, we ran up the hill ourselves with Wa-gu'li leading the way, shifting into his Indian gait, half running and half walking, gliding along like he had wings. Like a whippoorwill, perhaps? Yes, that's it, like a Wa-gu'li, which is what he is! Moving over the ground so gently yet so swiftly and smooth! I was amazed that, while I was breathing hard, Gu'li had no problem running out of breath. Even in a trot, he carried his head high with serenity, always breathing quietly.

We ran around behind Preacher Paul's house and heard Talking Rock knocking hard on the front door. Finally, the preacher's wife Christine came to the door. She said the head missionary was asleep and was not to be disturbed.

"*Wake him up, Miz Christine!*" Talking Rock said with his voice raised. "*We've got trouble!*"

We could hear through the front door. Preacher Paul got an ear full. Talking Rock was full of fury, telling him what had happened and that the evidence pointed to someone at the mission farm.

"*That's awful!*" the head missionary said, sounding downright disgusted. He agreed to go down shortly to Eu-har'lee to extend his regrets to the chief there.

Talking Rock turned around and headed back there to reveal his findings to Chief Ta-wa'di. Naturally, we tagged along behind.

"I saw enough sign on the trail and at the mission barn to convict somebody there," Talking Rock said. "I've got my suspicions as to who did it. I talked to Preacher Paul and we're going to find the culprit if it's the last thing we do."

# CHAPTER TWENTY-THREE

## The Conjurer Priests Conspire

That night the drums began beating right after sundown. Oak Tree said it was a war call. Whatever it was, it sounded dreadful, causing chills to run down my spine.

While we were sitting there on the steps of Wa-gu'li's cabin, we saw a stream of Cherokees walking along a nearby pathway and coming from different directions. Gu'li learned from Oak Tree that they were going to a meeting site just beyond Eu-har'lee near the Hi-wass'ee River. I could tell that they were priests, and Gu'li said they were going to another big talk being convened by A-sa'la, the Priest of Fire.

Su-ta'li recognized a lot of the aged men coming by.

They wore the signs of their rank, big necklaces with in-laid silver, and wide copper bracelets wrapped around their upper arms. All of them wore bright red, blue and gold bandanas cut out of cloth, imported from Augusta in exchange for deer skins. Gu'li told me also that the priests carried little buckskin pouches in which they carried their magic powders of alum and ground ginseng roots.

"And I see the priests are carrying in their right hands their most potent weapons," said Su-ta'li, "lightning rods."

"Lightning rods?" I asked.

"Yes, T'san. They're carved from the branches of trees struck by lightning."

"Holy damn!" I exclaimed.

"T'san, please watch your swearing!" Su-ta'li declared with a raised voice. "Your late mother and father never would have allowed it."

"I'm sorry, ma'am."

"About those lighting rods," Gu'li said, "you don't ever want to cause a priest to point one at you and call down a curse."

"What will happen?" I asked.

"Oak Tree says they can turn you into a witch, or maybe even worse, into a snake!"

I didn't have any more questions, but it was sure something to ponder. I also wondered if some of the conjurers were involved in witchcraft or sorcery. Pa had told me to be wary of people in the nation who might be involved in such. I decided I'd ask Talking Rock about it.

Gu'li said he was eager to slip through the mountains

again to spy on the priests and their Big Talk. "Why don't you go with me, T'san?" he suggested.

When I got back home, I asked Goliath Dan about it. He was as curious as I was to learn what was going on with the priests and he agreed to let me go. "Maybe you'll learn something that will be useful," he said.

"I hope so, Dan," I said. "It'll be a dark night. We're near the back of the moon now, so we'll probably have to camp out after the talk. Be too dark for us to walk home until morning."

Gu'li walked in about then. It was still light when we got started and we had enough light to easily make our way across to the ridges, off the trails. We traveled light. And carried in our pockets parched corn and beef jerky.

As soon as it got dark, the woods started humming with katydids and cicadas, all just buzzing away in a big chorus as we passed every waterway, plus deep notes from bull-frogs.

"Gu'li," I said, "do you get the feeling that the bugs and the frogs are singing back and forth to one another?"

"Yes, a lot of it is mating calls. And this time of the year, if we can stop and get quiet long enough, we might get to hear the mockingbird singing his night song!"

"In the middle of the night?"

"Yes. It comes at this time of the year. The mockingbird loves to sing in the dark of night, mocking other birds, and then he'll put on a big performance just before the sun rises."

We arrived just in time and found us a bushy spot on a hill overlooking the meeting site. The priests and head men were seated in the shape of a horseshoe.

The drums turned silent. A-sa'la walked up to the center of the ground next to where the fire was burning. He had on his beautiful cape of eagle feathers.

"Brothers," he said quietly, "it is time for serious talk. We are the inherited lawgivers of our nation, an honor that comes from years of tradition. Our sacred formulas and instruments were handed down to us from the Ad-hon'ski doctors of long ago. We must not allow this authority granted by the Great Spirit to slip from our hands. We will not permit our land and our people to be taken from us by the white missionary devils who're coming into our nation."

The priests grunted approval and beat their lightning rods against one another.

"A-sa'la is very sad and also angry tonight," Gu'li whispered. "I can feel the pain in his voice."

After a pause, the Priest of Fire continued:

"Brothers, hear me well: We are under threat; the white missionaries are dipping our people in our own absolution pools. It is a sacrilege, a stain on the memories of our greater fathers."

The priests stirred in their seats and grunted, seemingly in unison.

"Even some of our own brothers are becoming Jesus

God exhorters, preaching and linkstering for the missionary devils. It's time to put a stop to all this. We must bring these missionaries to the ground. They are turning our people from our old ways, from our sacred rites; they are demanding that we stop our dances and ball plays, and they say we can have only one wife."

Small laughs rustled through the ranks.

"They tell us that we must stop partaking of our black drink and even the white man's white whiskey! This we cannot accept."

"And now," he said with sadness in his voice, "they have burned one of our town houses, near here at Eu'har'lee."

The lightning rods went silent.

"Brothers, many of our wealthy blood kin are attempting to copy the white man. They wear fancy broadcloth and gingham. They teach their children to speak the white man's language. When they eat the beefsteaks from their cattle, they use iron forks and knives.

"And down on the big river plantations in Georgia, our wealthy mixed-breed brothers have become 'white Indians.' They have cut the trees and built big fields of cotton and corn and wheat. They have gangs of slaves and servants who drive them around in shiny carriages. They even have cats running around inside their homes!"

The priests hooted and hollered and clicked their rods. But A-sa'la's anger did not leave his face. Ordinarily a soft spoken, gentle person, his eyes and his voice blazed with fury. He raised his arms high for quiet. It was about here that he started using grunts—HA!—at the end of every thought, in the manner used by the Cherokee orators and exhorters now preaching the Jesus-God religion.

"When he starts with a HA grunt as if he is coughing it up from the bottom of his gut, he is getting real serious, he is speaking from the heart," I said.

Gu'li put his hand over my mouth. A-sa'la started up again.

"But my brothers, the worst—HA!—is coming from the white devil missionaries—HA!—They are bringing a new god to our people—HA!—one they call the Jesus God—HA! The one they say lived many moons ago across the great waters—HA! They want us to turn away from our own Great Spirit and accept their Jesus God—HA."

The circle of priests growled angrily. Then they saw that A-sa'la was eager to make another point and suddenly they grew quiet. This time, his voice dropped nearly to a whisper. We had to strain to hear.

"Brothers, we must inform our people of the real aim of the missionary devils."

Gu'li and I cupped our hands behind our ears. There was a long pause. "The missionaries have one aim," he said. "They are the advance men for the white man's government in Washington City to move us all toward the setting sun, brothers, across the Great Water into Ark-kan-saw—HA!"

Angry grunts rose from the crowd. "NO! NO! NO!," they yelled, rapping their rods.

"We must regain the souls of our people—HA!—We must stop the missionaries before it is too late—HA!—

*We must declare war*—HA!—and eliminate the mission-aries—HA!— starting with the one they call Preacher Paul—HA!"

We could tell that A-sa'la had the priests under his spell. We noticed something else. Some of the conjurers were gulping down white whiskey brought to them in gourds by their assistants, and they were shaking their rods in fury. A-sa'la paused to let them vent their anger, and he quickly took a swallow of the beverage that was brought to him by a runner.

"Now brothers," the Priest of Fire said, with his voice calming down, "the time has come to act. I have had talks with several local chiefs and here are the steps we must take, immediately:

"First, we must call on our people—HA!—no, *demand* of them—HA!—that they attend our sacred Cherokee religious meetings every seventh day, the one that the Una'kas call Sunday—HA! That is the day when our Cherokee traitors attend the Jesus-God churches—HA!

"We must hold our own traditional events on that day—HA!—and recapture our people and take them back from the missionaries."

"YES!" the priests yelled "YES! YES!"

"We will conduct our own services on those days—HA!—even ball plays, dances and the like—HA! If our people fail to attend—HA!—we will put curses on them and their families and their homes—HA!"

"YES, YES!" the priests yelled, clicking their rods. "We must announce our plans to our people—HA! Henceforth, to brothers whose family members violate our decrees, we will deny healing herbs and root medicines when they come to us—HA! And we must be extremely harsh on those brothers who attend Jesus-God services—HA!"

"YES! YES!" the priests yelled.

"We will call on some of our white friends for help—people such as *Ye'ni-hi*, Eph the whiskey man."

"YES! YES!"

"Now brothers, I come now to the most serious matter. Patrol guards, clear the grounds of all bystanders."

We crawled back in the laurels while the Cherokee troops circled the council ground, flushing out a few Cherokees and running them away, out of earshot. Wa-gu'li and I felt safe. We had plenty of cover in the woods. We held our ground, and A-sa'la started talking again, lowering his voice.

"Brothers, fellow priests, listen to my voice."

Now he was talking, not preaching, and he stopped using his "Ha!" grunts.

"In order to take back our nation, and our way of life, we must eliminate two of the missionary devils from our midst." Several priests grunted.

"I hereby appoint Walkin'stick and Rattlin'gourd to meet with *Ye'ni-hi* to find a way to resolve our difficulty. Your first and most important task will be to arrange the removal of the missionary devil called Preacher Paul and the number two man that they call Merlin the Missionary."

I couldn't believe what I was hearing, and Gu'li was as shocked as I was.

★   ★   ★

As the meeting was about to end, we walked away quickly and found us a grassy, open place on the nearby mountain bald to spend the night. It was a grand site, underneath a magnificent star-studded sky.

"The view is wonderful, Wa-gu'li, but where are we going to sleep?"

"Simple, T'san, we'll just pile us up some leaves from those oaks over there."

I don't know why I didn't think of it myself. The soft leaves made a wonderful pallet and shortly we got settled down and ate a bit of our dried corn and venison jerky.

It was a good while before we went off to sleep, thinking about what we had just heard. Some wolves started howling over on the next mountain range but we weren't afraid. "What do you think they're going to do to remove Preacher Paul and Merlin from our nation?" I asked.

"It's dreadful to even think about," Gu'li said, "but old man Coward will find a way, I regret to say."

"What would happen to the mission?"

"Hard to imagine," Gu'li said, "but the church's national leaders need to be told about Preacher Paul's severe new approach to the Cherokees. I've read The New Testament, the one that's been translated into Sequoyan talking leaves. The way I read it, the Jesus-God religious stands for love, not rigid harshness."

"That's the truth!" I said. "That's what Pa tried to relate in all of his sermons. He always said Christians are supposed to love people, particularly those who who have had a hard time of it like the Cherokees, and to be gentle with them."

As usual, Gu'li and I were in full agreement. But we sure worried and wondered what was going to happen next.

# CHAPTER TWENTY-FOUR

## Ephraim Coward gets a Proposition

I had learned a lot about Eph Coward—the one the Cherokees call *Ye'ni-hi*—due to our spying, and also when we accompanied him on the panther hunt. And I learned more in my talks with Talking Rock.

It was back in 1810, Talking Rock related to me, that Eph rode his horse to Henderson, Kentucky, and paid forty silver dollars for two young mules at a trading yard.

"When he arrived back in the valley with his strange animals," Goliath Dan said, 'They're half ass and half hoss!'" before going into a one of his roaring laughs with his head bouncing up and down on his thick neck."

Eph Coward disagreed: "These hyar gals, they's bred to

work, is what they air," he said in all seriousness as he patted the one he called Myrt on the shoulder.

I tried to contribute to the story. "For his trips around and about, I heard he adorned his mules with jingle bells strapped to their leather harness, like he did on the panther hunt."

"Actually the bells were suggested by Eph's wife, Dessie Mae Longwillow," Talking Rock said, "and Eph went along with the idea. He's the only person in this end of the Cherokee nation who owns mules. Most mountain Indians can't afford these gentle beasts of burden."

I came to learn that Ephraim Coward grew up as a rip-snorting youngster and a moonshiner, like his Scottish-Irish father and grandfather before him, but he held steadfast to his forebearers' love and admiration of the Cherokees.

Thus, Eph Coward, like his father before him, became a Cherokee citizen and took a Cherokee lass as his wife, I learned. "With his muscular arms," Gu'li told me, "he was recognized as being the champion hand wrestler in western North Carolina."

Gu'li also told me that while most Cherokees liked old *Ye'ni-hi*, those who knew him best, such as the conjurer priests, were aware that underneath his jovial personality resided a streak of violence that could explode at any time. "They knew that after a day of imbibing his own makin's,

Eph was unpredictable. At such times many made a point of avoiding him."

Eph was sitting on his front porch rocker when Conjurer Priests Walkin'stick and Rattlin'gourd walked up. Gu'li and I had heard from Oak Tree about the meeting and we were watching from nearby.

"Hello, brothers, take a seat," Eph offered in Cherokee. He signaled his cook Esther, a slender Creek woman, to bring each of the visitors a gourd containing the recipe.

"*Ana-Ye'ni-hi*—Mister Coward," said Walkin'stick. "I've known you a long time and I know your friendship to the Cherokee Nation. Our priests have held council," he continued. "We are all angry about the missionaries; they are corrupting our people and are sowing discord."

"Do tell," Eph said.

"Just recently, you may know, someone burned the Euhar'lee Town House, and we think the missionaries are behind it."

"Is that so?" Eph replied, appearing a bit shocked.

"Yes, sir," Walkin'stick said, "We are mainly concerned about the old one who wears a black hat and a black coat, the one they call Preacher Paul, and the young one who wears two feathers in his hair, and sometimes a turban, the one they call Merlin the Missionary."

"Yep, I know 'em both," said the old man, letting loose a volley of tobacco juice in a stream that arched into a bush off the porch. "Yeah, old Merlin is a nice feller and he's been atter me. Preaches about the sins of drinkin'. Been atter my wife Dessie Mae, too, and her sister, askin' them to jine the church and get their selves dipped in Persimmon Creek."

"Really?" Rattlin'gourd replied.

"Yes sir-ee. Merlin promised them if they will repent of their past bad deeds and trust in Jesus Christ, that they can come out of the water as new people, free of sin."

"And what do you say to that?" Walking'stick asked.

"I'm right dubious, if you ask me, fellers."

We could see Walkin'stick and Rattlin'gourd grinning big, knowing they were talking to a soul brother.

"Now Preacher Paul is a different man altogether, right haughty, and a distant feller, while Merlin is a likable sort and right accommodatin'. But don't git me wrong, Merlin's barkin' up the wrong tree when he talks down the recipe. You know as well as I do, Walking'stick, that it's good for you as a medicine and otherwise, provided you don't abuse it and become a sot like some people have done."

"Well said, brother," Walkin'stick replied with a boozy belch.

"Let's get down to the real business of our visit," said Rattlin'gourd. "The Ad-hon'ski Council wants you to help us remove both of the missionary preachers."

"Remove them?"

"Yes."

"Even Merlin?" Coward asked.

"Yes, we've got to get him out of the nation. Him and Preacher Paul."

"Really?"

"Well, yes, whatever it takes to remove them from our borders. What do you suggest?"

"Burn 'um out."

"What did you say, sir?"

"Burn them out. Just set their mission houses a'farr. I could get someone to do it in the middle of the night."

"No!" Walkin'stick said firmly. "That's out of the question. We don't want to risk harming any of the young scholars. Some of them could get killed if the fire spread."

"All right, then, why not threaten them once or twice that you will throw them into the river if they don't leave? If they don't hightail it out of there pretty soon after, just toss 'em into Persimmon Creek during a heavy downpour…let 'em wash down to the ocean."

"Could you help us do that?"

"I think I could arrange it…"

# CHAPTER TWENTY-FIVE

### The River Toss
*(After an Unfortunate Ball Play)*

A Cherokee ball play is a wondrous thing to watch. My first experience seeing such a spectacle took place sometime ago at the Indian frolic ground at Nottley. Talking Rock took Gu'li and me there, and such violent knocking of bodies together, along with gnashing of teeth and breaking of bones, came as a pure revelation to me, far beyond anything I had ever witnessed in my lifetime.

I guess the reason that the game between *Ta-ma'li* and *Ay-uh'wa'si* went so ferocious that day, to my eyes, was on account of all the wagering going on. One Cherokee bet all of his clothing, including the deerskin coat on his back, plus his woman. Poor fellow lost his wife and all his duds that day, when *Ay-uh'wa'si* won.

Well sir, that first ball play I'd ever seen was recollected to my mind Sunday morning while Gu'li and I sat quietly in the Eu-har'lee Mission Church, attending the Sabbath services along with Wa-gu'li's ma, Su-ta'li. The small church, built of logs, was not far from the charred remains of the burned out Town House, and that's the reason we went down there to worship with the local people, to show our support.

I couldn't believe my eyes hardly when, just as we started singing a hymn, I saw through the window the beginning of a ball play right there next to the church, on this, the holy day of the week!

Gu'li and I had a good view since we were sitting on the log bench right next to a right hand window near the back that looked out on to the open space of hard ground. Gu'li whispered to me that that was where Cherokee children often played chunky games, rolling round rocks to see who could come closest to the mark.

Through the window I saw Cherokee young men trooping up, two whole teams of players getting ready to start play. Their backs had been properly scratched by a priest and the bloody gashes were plain to see. Gu'li had told me the players are first led into the water for a holy talking-to by the priest, following which they get their backs scratched with bear claws. Then, he said, with blood streaming down their backs, the players usually wade deeper into the stream and wash off most of the blood before they run out to the ball field.

On this day, the players were tall fellows whose muscles glistened in the sunshine, and whose straight black hair shined like silk. They all possessed fine-looking faces with high cheek-bones, small hawkish noses, and dark brown and black eyes, brimming with smartness.

When the players took the opening toss and started slapping and tackling and kicking and gouging one another as they fought over that little ball of deer hair, and started screaming and hollering, Preacher Paul laid down his Bible and took notice. So did the folks in church.

It was an athletic melee' for sure and I mean a big one, what Hawkeye would call a Tug of War. The first thing that flashed through my mind was: *The priests are behind this. It's their reply to the torching of the Eu-har'lee Town House.* And I wondered if this was just the beginning.

Actually, I thought this near-naked play on a Sunday was not nearly as bad as what had been done to the Cherokees, the burning down of the Eu-har'lee Town House. But Preacher Paul didn't take it that way and he resumed preaching.

Pretty soon, nobody much in the church was paying attention to him. Loud whispering broke out among the worshipers, and several of the Cherokee young people on the back logs ran outside to witness the spectacle.

Finally, Preacher Paul closed his Bible. "Brothers and sisters," he said, "this is sacrilegious, an abomination! May the Lord strike the players dead, every one of them who are taking the Sabbath in vain and showing off themselves in their sinful way here in this holy place. They are flaunt-

ing their heathenism in our faces and God will not countenance it." He yelled to his linkster exhorter to go out and
relay his strong displeasure at what was going on outside.

None of the players fell dead; instead they became more
rowdy and boisterous, so Preacher Paul prayed a short
prayer and dismissed his congregation, what was left of
them.

Su-ta'li wanted to go straight on home, saying she didn't
need to witness any more such carrying on. As she hurried
out, she kept her eyes looking straight ahead. Gu'li and I
walked most of the way home with her, but as soon as we
could break free, we turned around and ran back to see
what else was happening at Eu-har'lee.

When we returned, we found a bunch of folks on both
sides of the field, some of them church members, mostly
the menfolk and youngsters. Gu'li and I started climbing a
Shagbark Hickory tree at one end of the field for a better
view.

"What are you boys doing?" came a voice from behind.

We turned and were awful relieved when we saw it was
Goliath Dan Haughton.

"We're trying to climb to a high-up seat," I said.

"Did you just get here?" he asked.

"No. We're just back from walking Su-ta'li home."

"Well, T'san, you and Gu'li should have been here right
after the church service ended."

"Why?" I asked.

"Well, Preacher Paul came roaring out of the church house with his black hat on, in a terrible tizzy, trailed by Caleb Clark.

"The preacher went straight out into the middle of the athletes, saying the wrath of God was going to descend on them and he tried to break up the game.

"What happened next, the players *dee*-scended on the two of them, picked them up, one under each arm and leg, and deposited them on to the rostrum and dared them to interfere in the ball play any more."

"Then what did Preacher Paul do?" That was me asking.

"Last I saw, he and Caleb left from the back door and were high-tailing up the trail back to the mission."

The ball play didn't last long after that. When the Deer Clan's star player, *Wa-la-si'yi* (Giant Frog), ran the ball to the goal, and made another score for a total of twelve, the referee raised his hand and called the game. Gu'li and I agreed that it was clear the ball play there on a Sunday was meant to shame Preacher Paul for the town house burning, although we knew he was innocent.

"It's a shame that many Cherokees have already blamed the cowardly act on all the missionaries," I said, "particularly Preacher Paul, who I think was sincerely saddened like most of the other missionaries, and was trying his best to pinpoint and punish the arsonist."

The head missionary didn't let up on his war against the conjurer priests, calling them infidels and heathens, and urging his dwindling church membership to band together and oppose such behavior.

We got the feeling that the tension between Preacher Paul and the priests was rapidly coming to a head and that someone was going to get hurt.

One day Gu'li heard the priests had sent a message to Preacher Paul threatening to throw him into the river unless he relented and allowed them to practice their own religion in their own way and the same for them to hold festivals, night dancing and the ball play.

Instead of relenting, Preacher Paul got on his horse and rode from village to village, delivering his sermons everywhere he could get an audience. Merlin was doing the same thing, of course, but couching his messages in a more loving, gentle tone.

A week later, during a drippy, dark, overcast day that followed a heavy rainstorm, the missionary suffered a terrible fate. The story came to us from our friend Oak Tree, who was walking by. He said Preacher Paul was riding his brown roan on his way to Tuk-se'gee when he was stopped on the trail by two half-breeds. According to Oak, the two eldest Coward sons, Faron and Abe, were involved and were accompanied by The Thunder, a conjurer priest.

"The missionary's horse nearly threw him when the men

blocked his way," Oak Tree told us in Cherokee, with Gu'li linkstering. "Abe grabbed the roan's bridle and held on while his brother Faron pulled out a pet rattlesnake from a box and stuck its head into Preacher Paul's face."

Oak related the rest of the confrontation:

"'Git down off yer hoss, Preacher, and be quick about it,' Faron said, 'else I'm gonna turn this rattler loose on ye.'

'Now take it easy, men,' the missionary said, as quoted by Oak Tree, 'Don't do anything rash.'

Oak Tree recalled that, as Preacher Paul swung down off his horse, he said, 'Men, you know the wages of sin is death…woe be unto them that defy the Lord. His wrath is powerful and mighty.'

'Save your sermons for someone else, Preacher Paul,' Abe Coward said, slapping the roan on his rump. 'You ain't got no wrath to turn loose on nobody.'

'Wait a minute, men, don't let that horse get away. That saddlebag's got my Bible in it, and my sermon notes . . .'

'You won't be needin' them, Missionary,' Faron said as he tucked his rattler back in the box. The two grabbed hold of the old missionary by his arms and walked him down to the banks of the Persimmon Creek, where he had immersed so many of his converts.

'What are you aiming to do?' Preacher Paul asked.

'Just you wait and see,' Faron Coward said.

'You're not going to carry out the threat I received from the priests, are you?'

There was a pause, and Faron said, 'The Cherokees tell me ye're gettin' too big fer your britches, pastor. Have you read in your Bible about Old Testament revenge? A eye for a eye and a tooth for a tooth?'

'Of course. Who hasn't?'

'Well, old man, you gon'a find out what it's like to be on the receivin' end of that revenge for burning the Eu-har'lee Town House.'

'Wait a minute, men, I had nothing to do with that burning,' replied Preacher Paul."

Oak Tree said at that point the rained-soaked boys walked their captive onto a big rock that jutted out at a wide stretch of the creek, the very place which had served over the years as the priests' absolution pool and which the missionaries used for their baptisms.

The creek was roaring angry, Oak Tree said, and the water was overflowing its banks from the thunderous rainstorm, along with lightning and booming thunder.

"All right now, missionary," Faron Coward said. "We're gonna give you a little baptizin'!"

Oak Tree said the young men first wrapped cowhide ropes around the missionary's hands and ankles, and then lifted him by his arms and legs and swung him back and forth and, on the count of three, with a WHOOP, sent him hurtling into the air way out into the roaring stream, right into the deep pool. Abe picked Preacher Paul's black felt hat from the ground and sailed it out onto the water, and it spun around on the surface, striking a rock and moving on downstream, not too far behind the preacher.

The way Oak Tree told it, the young men roared with laughter as they watched the old missionary go under the

water and then watched as he bobbed up one time farther downstream. He went under again and never came up
any more in their line of vision. They clapped their hands
in glee, knowing that the conjurer priests would be well
pleased.

As they turned to get on their horses, Abe Coward
turned to the conjurer observer and said, 'Well, Thunder,
was that to your likin'?'

'Good throw, Abe. And you too Faron. Very good throw.
We might want to put you two on one of our ball teams.'

Faron Coward started to mount his horse and declared,
'Well, Thunder, I reckon you and the Priest of Fire won't
have to worry no more about the old pale face preacher
man.'

'That's the truth,' The Thunder said.

Oak Tree said that as the men were leaving the scene, a
bolt of lightning struck a poplar tree near them, causing
their horses to dash down the trail, leaving the Cowards
partly paralyzed for a few minutes. Then the thunderstorm
deluge turned even worse.

Well sir, after hearing the whole story from Oak Tree,
my heart beat many beats of sympathy for the old missionary. Everyone knew Preacher Paul to be a tough old cod-
ger, strict and demanding, but there was no doubt he was
sincere and had a strong faith in God and was no doubt
innocent of any involvement in the Eu-har'lee burning.

"It's so sad," I told Gu'li, "*Why did the priests have to do this to him?* Especially since nobody much believed he was personally responsible for the town house fire?"

"T'san, you and I know it wasn't Preacher Paul that lit that fire, but that old man Clark was the likely one. I think he probably did it in an attempt to please the head missionary in his controversy with the priests."

When we got back and told Dan and Kindness the story, they were shocked.

Talking Rock was there also. "How awful," he said. "We need to pray for Preacher Paul. The only way he can survive will be with a miracle from God almighty. We need to pray for a miracle."

So we held hands and prayed and asked the Lord to help Preacher Paul survive his awful predicament.

Although the head missionary was not one of my favorite people, I took time to pray again for him when I got home. Gu'li told me he would do the same in the Cherokee way, and would ask Su-ta'li to pray for him also.

I suddenly thought about Merlin. I hadn't seen him around for a couple of days. I wondered—*Lord have mercy!*—did he suffer the same fate as Preacher Paul? I had a hard time getting to sleep, thinking about Merlin. I got back down on my knees and prayed again, asking God to please help him escape the awful fate that had come to Preacher Paul.

# CHAPTER 26

## Preacher Paul's River Ride

A bruised and battered Preacher Paul was tumbling down Persimmon Creek like flotsam, trying to keep his head above water and attempting to suck enough oxygen into his lungs to stay alive.

The water surged in giant foamy waves, pitching him from crest to crest. He kept thinking that this was the end time for him, rising on a bumpy elevator to heaven as it were. He kept repeating the lines of the 23rd Psalm:

> *Yea though I walk through the valley of*
> *the shadow of death, I shall fear no evil*

The head missionary was obviously out of his head, having a terrible time of it as he bobbled down the waterway, smacking into rocks while being swept by the churning river and its strong thunderstorm current. He kept trying to remember what had led him to this awful predicament. His clothes were in shreds, torn to tatters, and his precious black hat was nowhere to be seen. Fortunately, the rawhide strips tied to his hands and feet had been cut on jagged rocks and he had gained freedom of movement, enabling him to try to swim. He grabbed a root and pulled himself up to a bank, where he rested for several hours until the bank crumbled and he fell back in the water.

Down into a deep pool he plunged, holding his breath seemingly for an eternity, until at last he was tossed to the surface again. That enabled him to gulp in huge gasps of air. The roar of the thunder and lightning and the heavy raindrops beat on his ear drums, and his head was spinning like a top.

Amid all the tumult, he kept trying to recall, *How did I get into this awful cauldron of angry water and sharp rocks?* He remembered the big thunderstorm coming up and something about a church member who needed him, the Cherokee Maggie, wife of The Turtle, who was about to die. And then he recalled being faced by a rattlesnake.

But how did he fall into this devilish river? Surely a product of Satan. His attempt to reconstruct it all in his battered mind ended abruptly as he crashed into a big boulder, crunching his right shoulder and elbow. A surge tossed him high over the rocks and plunged him down into a deep pool. Then he found himself floating on his back. Overhead was a cool canopy of trees and occasionally a tiny patch of sky in the black overcast. But his good fortune didn't last long. Next he found himself swept against a rocky bank.

Later on the first day, the missionary grabbed hold of some roots and pulled up on the bank and lay down and slept for several hours, maybe all day. But during the night, the bank crumbled again and he rolled back down into the turbulent water of a dark night.

*A-sa'la, the Priest of Fire, stood by the roaring Hi-wass'ee, chanting to the Great Spirit, and happy that his missionary nemesis was gone forever. Suddenly he saw a vision—that of white missionaries and all Una'kas being themselves run out of the Cherokee Nation, returning the country to the way it had been in earlier years. Giving back to the Cherokees their ancient homeland with its seven clans, its happy festivals, its ball plays and dances as in the olden days. And leaving its people in their villages and creek-side farms near the bones of their ancestors on the hillsides. A smile creased his face and he felt good about the thought. A Cherokee Nation restored to its ancient glory, to the days before the white man came in and spoiled it all.*

It was the second day now and Preacher Paul grabbed and held to a hickory root in quiet desperation, mumbling, "I shall fear no evil for thou art with me…"

Then he felt something pulling him up and glimpsed through his one good eye the firm grasp of a hand on his wrist. Next he found himself up on a flat rock. He was half blind, with one eye shut tight and he wondered who or what had brought him out of the water. He shook his head trying to clear the water from his good eye.

"Where am I?" Preacher Paul mumbled in a whisper.

A-sa'la's eyeballs turned white and he jumped back. He had thought he had pulled up a drowning Cherokee, but it looked a lot like the head missionary who was supposed to be long gone down the River Hi-wass'ee.

"Preacher Paul?" he said to the man lying prostate on the rock. The old missionary nodded, but only slightly. He was still gasping for breath, panting hard. He was hardly recognizable; his face was a bloody pulp and blood was oozing from cuts all over his body, his hands, shoulders, back and elbows.

Looking down at the bleeding Jesus-God preacher, the Priest of Fire suddenly felt a bit of compassion for the man whom he had hated for so many moons. As he watched the missionary's chest rising and falling with each breath, he asked himself, "*How was it that Preacher Paul was delivered right to our sacred pool here on the Hi-wass'ee?*" And how would he explain it to the other priests? Would they believe him should he tell them he thought he was rescuing a member of his own tribe? Or should he push the hated missionary back into the river, to die a certain death?

"Missionary!!" A-sa'la yelled into Preacher Paul's face. He lifted him by his shoulders and shook him, seeking without success to ask him a question. Then he gently laid the old missionary back down on the flat rock on his back.

The rains had stopped and Wa-gu'li and I were walking down to the river Hi-wass'ee, glad to be out after the days of awful thunderstorms. When we walked down past A-sa'la's cabin we saw him squatting on a flat rock surrounded by the river. I noticed he was holding the arm of what appeared to be a bloody body. We hastened down and followed the trail across to the rock.

"It's Preacher Paul!" Wa-gu'li yelled as we got closer.

"It shore is!" I screamed, using one of Goliath Dan's favorite words, and looking at the man we thought had been washed out to sea.

"*Is he alive?*" Gu'li asked the chief priest in Cherokee.

"Yes, he's breathing," A-sa'la said quietly. "But he needs attention. Wa-gu'li! Please go fetch some help. We need to get him up to my cabin."

Gu'li sped away.

I inched up closer. It was Preacher Paul all right. His bushy red eyebrows and red hair were still there, but plastered down with blood. I couldn't take my eyes off him. Boy was he cut up. Blood was oozing from bruises and forming scabs over his head, shoulders, chest, back and elbows.

I felt sadness and pity for the old guy.

Just as Corn Silk walked up, having run into Wa-gu'li, the missionary regained consciousness again. He didn't open his eyes, but started mumbling.

*"Yea though I walk through the valley of death, I shall fear no evil . . . I am falling, falling, falling, into a deep pool. I must hold my breath . . . This is my end time."*

A-sa'la got him to sit up briefly, then Preacher Paul fainted again and went limp and the priest lowered him back down onto the rock.

I was amazed at the tenderness shown by the Priest of Fire toward his old enemy. "You rescued him just in time, sir," I said.

With Corn Silk linkstering, A-sa'la said, "I pulled him out, sure, but it must have been his God that kept him alive all that time. How he survived in the onrushing thunderstorm waters is a total mystery."

The old missionary started mumbling again.

"What is he saying, Corn Silk?" I asked.

"He's having a nightmare. He says he is falling into a deep pool of water."

"A nightmare?" A-sa'la asked, hearing Corn Silk's statement in Cherokee.

"Yes," I said, "he's dreaming a dreadful dream…repeating all of the horrors of his awful trip down the river."

*"Must hold my breath . . . Water is deep . . . my chest will burst . . ."*

"You're right, T'san," A-sa'la said, with Corn Silk translating. "He's purging the terrible memories from his soul.

Once he dreams it, he should be partly free of it, the memories won't bother him so much any more."

"You are very wise, A-sa'la Car-tee'kee," I said.

The missionary started mumbling again, in rambling sentences:

"*. . . Oh my head . . . I'm whirling . . . spinning like a buggy wheel, out of control . . . I shall fear no evil, for thou art with me . . . thy rod and staff, they protect me . . . oh! the roar of the river, it is beating on my brains! Lord God, what did I do to receive this punishment? . . . *"

He dropped off into a deep sleep again and A-sa'la picked up his right hand and examined his fingers that were bleeding. Then he reached over and placed his turban under the old man's head to make him more comfortable.

"He's no bigger than I am," the priest said, as if discovering something new. "And he has many of the features of the Cherokee. He has long, thinning red hair and naturally his skin is pale. Otherwise, he looks like our own people."

I could see plain that the head priest was stunned.

Gu'li came back with two young villagers. They placed the old missionary on a deerskin litter and helped Corn Silk and me lug him out of the river and up through the laurels to A-sa'la's cabin.

"Place him on that table," A-sa'la said. It was in his yard under an oak tree. Then he brought out a bearskin to cover the beaten old man who probably was chilled from two days' exposure in the stormy downpour.

A fellow conjurer, Toon-e'wah, rushed up after hearing the news. Together they cleaned off the missionary's wounds and applied herbs and salves and gave him a gourd of water.

"The priests will want to question Preacher Paul," Toon-e'wah said. "Particularly since it was they who had condemned him to death. I'll get a runner to assemble them here so we can decide what to do."

"Thank you," A-sa'la said.

The Priest of Fire brought out a chair and took a seat next to the table. But, every few minutes, he would lift up the bearskin to check on the missionary's breathing.

I decided to ask A-sa'la a question about our friend Merlin.

"A-sa'la Car-te'kee, sir," I said. "We heard you spared the life of Merlin the Missionary. Why? He probably persuaded many more Cherokees to become Christians in recent months than Preacher Paul."

"It was simple," he replied with Gu'li linkstering. "We reconsidered and instructed Eph Coward to leave Merlin alone. Merlin had been very kind and helpful to so many of our people and had been acting more like a Cherokee than a white missionary."

*Well didn't that beat all!*

Gu'li and I decided to go home to rest a while, and come back later to see what the priests would do with the old missionary now that he was still alive, although awful beat up, and just about dead.

"Merlin might like to come back with us," Gu'li said.

# CHAPTER TWENTY-SEVEN

## The Trial of Preacher Paul

Wa-gu'li and I found us a good spying spot on a nearby hillside when the priests began the trial of Preacher Paul. We arrived there just as they were lighting the torches.

"Is that the missionary there under the bearskin?" The Thunder asked as he walked up.

"Yes," said the Priest of Fire.

After a long pause, the tall conjurer continued: "We've heard how you pulled him out of the river, A-sa'la, and saved his life. My question is, *why?*"

Several of the other newly arrived conjurers appeared to agree. Thus, even before poor old A-sa'la Car-tee'kee could call the meeting to order, he found himself facing a storm of scolding.

"My brothers, what else could I do?" A-sa'la asked. "I had prayed that the river would send the missionary to a drowning death. Instead, the river belches him up at my feet."

Gu'li and I were surprised when the old priest Dreadful Waters arose and pointed his lightning rod at the Priest of Fire.

"What else do you have to say, sir? Why did you rescue our worst enemy?"

"I have no answer," A-sa'la said, hanging his head, "other than that I first thought he was one of our own people about to drown. It was after I pulled him up that I recognized it was the missionary."

"Come now," Dreadful Waters said. "Would you have us believe that? You brought us here several days ago to join you in condemning the missionary to death. We voted to do just that. Now you have saved him. Perhaps we need to put **you** on trial."

The once-powerful Priest of Fire seemed to instantly lose his status as the Ad-hon'ski's chief priest.

Suddenly Preacher Paul coughed, flipped aside the bear-skin, rose up to a sitting position on the table, and looked around. It was almost like a ghost coming to life, but he was the awfulest looking ghost you could ever imagine. Splotches of red, blue and black covered his face and his body. His elbows and shoulders carried crusts of dried blood. Even his reddish hair was matted with blood and his right cheek and nose were bloody raw.

I could see that the priests were shocked that the old missionary—battered and wounded as he was—was still alive, and getting ready to talk!

For a few agonizing moments Preacher Paul and the priests gazed at one another without speaking. The croaking of the frogs could be heard along with the river itself, now receding from the rains.

The priests sat up straighter and several coughed. When Corn Silk arrived, A-sa'la asked him to stand next to the table to hold Preacher Paul and serve as linkster.

"Gentlemen," Preacher Paul said, clearing his throat, "I woke up a few minutes ago and heard some of your questions. Perhaps you will allow me to answer the main one that you had for A-sa'la." Corn Silk repeated his words in Cherokee.

"When A-sa'la pulled me from the awful river today, he did not recognize me at first, nor I him. He just happened to be alongside the stream for his early morning visit to the river. His act was merely one of charity, seeking only to help someone in distress. In our holy book, he would be described as the Good Samaritan, the man who stopped beside the road to help a wounded man. I am grateful to A-sa'la for his kindness.

"So, men of spirit, do not think that A-sa'la has betrayed you. Like you, he thought that I had long since drowned and had been washed out toward the sea."

There was a rustle in the circle, and I could tell that the conjurers were impressed. Some of the *Ad-hon'ski* priests whispered to one another, just as a few more priests arrived and took seats on the logs.

In spite of Preacher Paul's eloquent appeal, the holy men voted unanimously to go ahead ahead with a trial, to decide on his fate.

Tall Conjurer Priest Toon-e'wah strode to the front and took over the meeting, and in a deep-throated grunt, ordered A-sa'la to take a seat.

"At this time," Toon-e'wah said, "I wish to ask the missionary a few questions and then I will turn him over to the rest of you.

"Suppose we start at the beginning, Preacher Paul: Where did you come from? Where did you grow up as a boy?"

"I was born many miles from here, in the state of Maryland."

"And just when did your god anoint you as a missionary?"

"Sir, that's not the way it's done in our church. You see, I accepted Jesus Christ as my own savior as a young boy. Our young people are encouraged by their parents to become Christians, but it is a matter of exercising our own free will as to whether we will accept Jesus and believe in Him and worship Him, or whether we will become a nonbeliever."

"Ah, so some Un-a'kas don't believe in your god; is that so?"

"True. Those are people who are called atheists; their premise is that there is no supreme being. There are not many who reach that conclusion, I am happy to say."

"So while in your tender youth, you elected to become a believer in your god?"

"Yes, I guess I was around ten years of age. I reached the point where I trusted Christ as my savior, and the church in our village accepted me as a Christian and as a church member."

"Did your church then appoint you as a missionary?"

"No, I felt a call to become a minister and my church sent me off to school."

"You had a call?"

"Yes, one night I had a vision while I was praying—you know, talking to God with your eyes closed when…"

"You mean you talk to your god?"

"Oh, yes; did you not know that? We talk to our God all the time."

"And how do you do that?"

"Well, we study the scriptures in our Bible and then we kneel down beside the bed at night and at other times during the day and close our eyes and pray. We direct our prayers to our God. We ask for answers and sometimes He answers us quickly, and sometimes His answer comes along sometime later. But we must always be alert to hear His reply."

"You mean you hear him talking when he answers you?"

"Well, yes, it comes to my mind."

"What did he tell you?"

"I heard Him say that He wanted me to become a minister and to take the word of God to lost people around the world."

"Lost people?"

"Yes, people who do not know Christ."

"Oh, I see. People who do not worship your god?"

"Yes."

"So then what happened?"

"My church sent me to school in Providence, Rhode Island, to a seminary there."

"And what did you learn there?"

"I learned how to study to make myself approved of God."

"Did you win the approval of your god?"

"I graduated from the seminary, if that's what you mean. My professors gave me a divinity degree and I went back to Maryland."

"What happened then?"

"My church ordained me."

"What does that mean?"

"Well the deacons of our church, sort of like a group of beloved men, questioned me on my beliefs and found me qualified to become a minister."

"Then what happened?"

"They gathered around and laid hands on me and prayed for me and declared me ordained. Then they asked me to preach a sermon."

"So what did you preach about?"

"I took as my text John 3:16, 'For God so loved the world, that he gave his only begotten Son that whosoever believeth in him should not perish, but have everlasting life.'"

"What does that mean?"

"That means that if you believe in Christ Jesus, who is God's son, that you will live forever."

"You mean you won't die?"

"My body will die, yes, but if you're a born-again Christian, as I feel that I am, my spirit will live forever with God in heaven, along with my late wife and other Christians."

"Your wife was a Christian, was she?"

"Oh yes. She died the earthly death, but the real Eliza, her spirit, her soul, is living today with God in heaven. She shed her earthly body and left it here behind."

"So your wife's spirit is living with God in heaven?"

There was a stir across the circle of priests. Several sat up and cupped their ears to hear more clearly.

"Yes, that I believe. Her spirit, her mind and soul, are living with God today in Heaven. Like I said, I hope to join her some day."

"You mean you plan to live forever, too, your spirit, in your heaven?"

"That's correct. In God's heaven. That's what we believe, that's what happens to all good Christians who have confessed their sins and have accepted Christ as their savior."

Toon-e'wah seemed satisfied. "I am through with him for the time being," he said, motioning for someone else to ask questions of the old missionary. Toon-e'wah said it was time to take a brief break.

Corn Silk went to A-sa'la's spring and brought back a piggin of water along with a gourd. The missionary took several gulps then lay back down for a few minutes.

While the priests milled around, Gu'li whispered to me. "I wonder if Preacher Paul will be condemned and thrown back into the river again?"

"I don't know," I said, "but he sure is putting up a real fight. After hearing his initial testimony, I'm impressed. Maybe another miracle will happen."

Several more priests were awaiting their turn, and Gu'li said. "I'm praying Preacher Paul can keep on talking straight to them. We'll find out tonight if he can win his freedom and avoid another river toss."

I felt the same way. But I was still worried.

# CHAPTER TWENTY-EIGHT

### Just Who is Your God?

The trial got under way again and Corn Silk helped the weary missionary, who had been lying flat on the table, to sit up. The priest Sut'chee came forward with his lightning rod.

"Mister Missionary, just who is your god? You say you worship Jesus Christ but that he is the SON of god. How can you worship Jesus if it is his father who is your god?"

Preacher Paul attempted to get off the table again and almost fell to the ground. Corn Silk brought out a chair and the missionary flopped down on it. Then the linkster gave him a gourd of water.

"Actually we worship three Gods," Preacher Paul said.

"Three gods?" Sut'chee asked.

"Yes. The Father, the Son and the Holy Ghost. That's what we call The Trinity, three Gods in one."

"Explain that to me again," Sut'chee asked, looking a little puzzled.

"Well, it's this way, sir. We worship the Creator God, who is our supreme being. God sent His son to earth to live as a human being among men; this son was born of a virgin. His name was Jesus Christ. He was rejected and killed by man, the evil world, but after three days He rose from the tomb and now resides with God in heaven."

"What is the third god you worship?"

"The Holy Ghost. The Holy Spirit."

"And where does this holy ghost reside?"

"God's spirit resides everywhere . . . in heaven, on earth, in our hearts, our minds, our souls. He rode with me on my bumpy ride down the river, and I was praying to Him, talking with Him all the way. That is, when I was conscious, of course."

"You mean to tell me that part of your god resides within you?"

"That is true. Of course, we as Christians must pray and study to keep the Holy Ghost Spirit alive in us. Otherwise it might wither and die and a devil spirit could take its place."

"A devil spirit. You mean you believe there is a devil spirit?"

"I certainly do. Of course I hope I don't carry one in my soul, but there is such a thing, and if you don't keep your

Holy Ghost Spirit of godly love fortified and replenished daily, the devil spirit can take possession of your life. Yes, indeed. That's what causes people to do devilish things. They allow the evil spirit Satan to take control of them."

"Well, Mister Missionary, if I understand correctly, it seems to me that you people have a battle going on within yourselves all the time."

"That is true, Sut'chee, you are very insightful. Anyone who is human has such a struggle, a constant fight that goes on in our hearts and minds at all time, between good and evil, between God and the devil."

"Well, sir, how do you manage to stay out of the hands of the Satan devil?"

"We have the Bible, of course, which gives us God's word. We must constantly read it, and meditate on it, and continue to meditate on it and try to do God's will."

"Is that the black book we've seen you people carrying around?"

"Yes. Also we try our best to think and study on things true and pure. And, as I mentioned, we try to pray as often as we can, during the day, at meals and certainly before going to sleep at night."

"Has the devil Satan ever won control of you?"

"You want me to answer truthfully?"

"Of course we do."

Preacher Paul motioned for Corn Silk to bring him some more water and he delayed his answer until he could take a long drink from the gourd. He wiped off his lips with the back of his bruised hand.

"You asked if the Devil spirit ever got control of me. Well, I must confess that since my wife Eliza died, I have been tempted by the Devil. Indeed, I've had lust in my heart."

"Lust? I don't understand," the conjurer said, turning to Corn Silk, "Can you tell us the meaning?"

"I would defer to the missionary to define what he means," said Corn Silk.

"I regret to say that I have been tempted of the flesh," Preacher Paul said, standing up again. "I have thought about how nice it would be to sleep with one of your beautiful Cherokee maidens."

Muffled laughs broke out amongst the priests.

"Oh, so that is what you mean by the devil?" Sut'chee said. "I don't see how that's so reprehensible."

"It is not a small matter," the missionary said, lowering his head and lowering his voice.

"That's just one manifestation of how the Devil can take control of you. I have had a horrible struggle with it since Eliza died. It's easy to lose control to one's baser passions. That could lead to greater sins. And before long the Holy Spirit inside has given way to the Devil spirit."

Gu'li and I agreed that Sut'chee understood and appeared to show compassion for the battered old missionary.

"That's all the questions I have," he said. "For myself, I find the missionary guiltless. If we take a vote, I would vote to free him."

The priests seemed to be looking on Preacher Paul with new insight. Gu'li and I were both feeling that maybe he was not the devious hypocrite we had thought him to be. I got the feeling that the priests were considering him a mortal man much like them, subject to the weaknesses and whims of every man.

By this time, the missionary, weary, weak and wan, was about to fall again. Corn Silk grabbed him by the arm and the shoulder, and helped him into the chair. He also called for one of the bystanders to bring in another piggin of water.

"Thank you," Preacher Paul said, taking a long slurp from the gourd. "That sure is good water. Thank you kindly, Corn Silk."

The priest Terrapin Sitting Down arose and walked to the front, his lightning rod in his right hand.

"Mister Missionary, it appears to me that you Christians consider yourselves to be sons of god. Is that correct?"

"We are taught that we are made in God's image, if that is what you mean. And of course, we do carry God's spirit inside us, so long as we keep it nourished and alive and so long as we follow God's commandments."

"You don't look like a god to me," the priest said. "How can someone such as yourself be qualified to carry a god spirit inside your body?"

"That's one of God's promises to us," Preacher Paul said. "Even you, yourself, could become a carrier of the Christian God inside you, if you worked at it for a period of time."

"Me, a Cherokee priest, could carry within my head the spirit of the Jesus Christ god?"

"Yes, of course. There are many Cherokee Christians throughout your nation. Their bodies are vessels that carry the Jesus Christ spirit inside them. You need to talk to some of them, such as Sister Su-ta'li. Perhaps you, too, would see fit sometime to come join our class of instruction on how to become a Christian."

Terrapin Sitting Down began shaking his head.

Taking up another subject, he said, "It appears you missionaries think that you know it all as far as gods are concerned. What I want to know is, why don't you, Preacher Paul, and the other missionaries, show some respect for our Great Spirit? And why don't you show respect for our Cherokee traditions?"

"I apologize to you, sir," Preacher Paul said, "if I have failed to show respect to you and Cherokees generally. I regret that I have acted arrogant in recent times. I certainly have an affection for the Cherokee people."

"Preacher Paul, you have forced many of our people to quit our Cherokee traditions such as our festivals and dances and the ball play. Because of you we are losing the traditions and discipline of our forefathers.

"And besides that, we are extremely upset that you are polluting our holy rivers and creeks where our people for centuries have gone to the absolution pools to cleanse their souls. Why do you defile our waterways with your baptizing? And why did you tell your members you would banish those Cherokees who refused to follow your edict?"

"I apologize for doing that. I guess I allowed the angry Satan spirit to get to me recently. For your information, I recently saw the error of my ways, thanks to counsel from Missionary Merlin, and I destroyed that proclamation the day before I was tossed into the river."

Terrapin Sitting Down appeared to be somewhat pacified, then took up another subject. "Sir, we are greatly in fear of the white tide that surrounds us and the Un-a'ka governments in Washington and Georgia which are plotting to move us toward the setting sun. That is another reason we are angry with you missionaries and your Jesus God. We have our own Great Spirit who meets our needs completely."

Preacher Paul paused briefly and rose from his chair. "We don't seek to force anyone to switch his allegiance to our God," he said, "but we do try very hard to persuade people to join us in worshiping the true God."

"*The true god?*" Terrapin Sitting Down mocked. "How can you stand there and tell me your god is the true god?"

"Because we have evidence that He is really the true God."

"What evidence?"

"Our Bible gives us a list of witnesses who knew God's son Jesus, who came to earth as a human being. His disciples, Matthew, Mark, Luke and John, and Peter and others, walked with Jesus and witnessed His being on earth and His being hung on the cross to die. These witnesses saw Him after He rose from the dead and walked among men for some time before ascending to heaven to be with His heavenly Father."

"Is that so, now?"

"Yes. Like I just said; it's recorded in our Bible, in our holy talking leaves."

Preacher Paul then asked Corn Silk if he had a Bible handy. The linkster pulled out his New Testament printed in the Sequoyan syllabary.

"Would you please read him some passages from Matthew about the time Jesus was walking among men before and after rising from the dead?" Corn Silk read the passages about Jesus' resurrection from the tomb. The priests listened intently.

"But how do you know this is true?" Terrapin Sitting Down asked.

"Because this is the word of God," the missionary said, lifting up the Bible. "The disciples witnessed Jesus on earth, witnessed His death, and then witnessed His returning to life and later His ascension to heaven. They recorded their eyewitness accounts which are part of our Bible's New Testament. Copies of this New Testament in Talking Leaves are available to all Cherokees who wish one."

Terrapin Sitting Down took his seat and the priest All

Bones came forward. "Mister Missionary, you say when you received your calling to be a preacher for your god, you felt called to rescue lost people. Is that the reason you have come here in our midst? Do you consider the Cherokees to be lost?"

"Well, yes sir, some Cherokees are, according to our definition."

"Please elaborate."

"It's through no fault of your own, sir. It's just that many of the people in this part of the Cherokee nation have never had the opportunity to hear about our God, and therefore we, by our definition, would consider them lost."

"So you have come to rescue us, is that it?"

"Well, yes, that is our mission, to find lost souls and to help them learn about the true God."

"So what do you want to do, now that you have found all of us 'lost people'?"

"We've been trying our best to bring you God's message—that of love and reconciliation, salvation and eternal life."

"Eternal life. Explain that once more."

"Well, our God has the capability of giving you eternal life if you renounce your past sins, confess those sins and ask for forgiveness."

"It's that easy, is it?"

"Yes sir, it's rather simple; we are pleased that many Cherokees in your nation have taken the simple steps to commit themselves to our God and to our faith."

All Bones swung around and prepared to ask more questions. "Mister Missionary, is it not a fact that you and all the missionaries are merely preparing our people for removal to the land of the setting sun?"

"Absolutely not, far from it! " Preacher Paul said, seemingly getting his breath anew. "The truth is that we missionaries side with those of you who want to stay here in your ancient homeland. All missionaries sincerely support you in your wish to stay in your homeland, here where lie the bones of your ancestors. A number of the Presbyterian missionaries have been dragged down to jail in Georgia because they support the Cherokees' wish to remain in their nation. I myself and the other missionaries are prepared to help you fight for your rights in that regard. Only one missionary that I know of, in Georgia, supports the idea of moving west. As you may know, he and his church mmbers are going voluntarily to Arkansas."

"If it is true that you wish for us to remain here," All Bones asked, "why do you persist in trying to take away our traditions—even trying to abolish our language? And the ball play?"

"I regret that we have been so aggressive as regard to your folkways. And as far as the ball play, we feel it has created more problems for you such as gambling and whiskey-drinking. These are Devil gods that can take hold of your souls. So we oppose the ball play unless it is cleaned up with the removal of moonshine whiskey and the pernicious gambling that accompany the sport.

"And of course," he added, "we challenge your worship of your surroundings…the rivers and trees and animals."

"Why is this so?"

"Well, we believe in a living God, Christ Jesus, whom I told you about, who lived here on earth and died the cruel death on the cross for our sins. He lives today in our hearts. So it is so that it is Jesus we worship along with the Father God, and the Holy Spirit, not the rivers and the animals, for instance."

"One more question," All Bones said.

"Can you assure us that none of the missionaries are conspiring to prepare us for our removal?"

"Absolutely," Preacher Paul said. "As I mentioned earlier, I and all the missionaries here in your nation are prepared to put our lives on the line to stand with you to prevent the politicians in Washington from pushing you out of your homeland."

"If you can permit me asking an additional question," All Bones said, "explain to us the burning of the Eu-har'lee Council House."

"Our mission organization and I personally had absolutely nothing to do with setting the place afire and we regret exceedingly that this happened. We think we have identified the perpetrator of this dastardly deed, and we plan to press charges that will send him to jail."

"That's all the questions I have," All Bones said. "From what I have heard from the lips of the missionary, I do not think he is guilty of our charges. I would vote to let him go."

And so it went. By the time the final priest finished with his questioning, the consensus appeared strong in the missionary's favor.

Dreadful Waters stood up spoke for many of the priests: "In my opinion, gentlemen, this man, Preacher Paul, has a clean and innocent heart. For me, I say, give him his freedom."

Although Thunder was still adamant that the head missionary should be thrown back into the river, the priests, by seven to one, voted to turn him loose. And well it was, because Preacher Paul was about to collapse from fatigue, and shivering from the chills.

After the priests left, we sat for a while on the hillside and wondered what would happen next.

We took another look and wondered what was going to happen to A'sa-la. He seemed saddened and tired, deserted by the other priests and now left alone with his former adversary. And we also worried about Preacher Paul who was still hanging on to life there on the table. Corn Silk seemed puzzled also as to what he needed to do.

"They need help," I told Gu'li. "Maybe we can get Merlin and some others to help us out."

# CHAPTER TWENTY-NINE

### Preacher Paul Recovers, Caleb Clark Confesses, and A Eu-har'lee House-Raising

Well sir, even the folks who weren't the fondest followers of Preacher Paul silently cheered when the crusty old
missionary was set free. One of them, Su-ta'li, rushed to
A-sa'la's cabin directly after the trial to see what she could
do to help.

As she walked up, Preacher Paul fainted again and fell
flat on his face for the third time.

"Hey, T'san," Corn Silk yelled, "come help me lift the
missionary back up onto the table." Which I was eager to
do. Then Su-ta'li asked the Priest of Fire if Preacher Paul
could be taken inside his home.

"Yes," A-sa'la said. "Bring him in here and put him on my bed." *Wonder of Wonders*, I thought to myself, *what a splendid gesture, a miracle unto itself!*

Su-ta'li moved right in and took over the care of the wounded missionary and asked us to be gentle bringing him in. She fluffed up a turkey feather pillow on which to lay his head.

"What Preacher Paul needs is rest," she said and asked A-sa'la's wife Sun-a'lee to heat up a pot of sassafras tea. "And would you also please bring me a gourd of the apple recipe?" she asked in Cherokee. "We need to clean up the missionary's wounds."

Taking a cloth, Su-ta'li soaked it with the recipe and massaged the missionary's brow, cheeks and nose. Then she re-cleaned the cuts that covered his face, chest and elbows, and applied fresh root ointments.

I smelled the recipe right off. It enveloped the room with a strong aroma of apples. The missionary woke up for a minute, winced at the smells, then fell back to sleep.

"We need to wake him up in an hour or so," Su-ta'li said, "so we can get a little food in him, maybe some soup. But for now he needs to get some sleep."

Three quarters of an hour later, as she sat beside the bed, reciting Bible verses, the old missionary woke up mumbling. "Where am I?" he asked.

"Rest easy, Preacher Paul. It's Su-ta'li. You were pulled from the river by A-sa'la; the *Ad-hon'ski* priests put you on trial and they voted to turn you loose. You are free. You can continue your missionary work across the valley."

"Where am I?" he asked again.

"You're in A-sa'la's cabin, the chief priest. He's sitting outside and would like to talk to you when you're ready."

"Oh, he does?"

"Yes. He says he's quitting his life as a conjurer priest. I believe he wishes to go to your anxious bench when you're ready to preach again."

"Oh my goodness! Praise be to God."

"Don't count on converting many more of the *Ad-hon'ski*, sir. The Thunder and his like are still angry that you didn't drown in the river like they intended you to do in the first place."

"That's too bad. We'll just have to work harder." Then he slumped back into sleep.

✯ ✯ ✯

About that time, Merlin walked up and I gave him a bear hug since I was so happy to see him alive and well.

"Thanks for all of your prayers, T'san," he said. "I heard you all were praying for me after the Preacher Paul incident."

"Gu'li and I were concerned that the priests might have had you tossed in the creek also," I said.

"Praise the Lord that they changed their minds," he replied. "Is Preacher Paul all right?"

"As well as could be expected," Corn Silk replied. "He's fainted several times since A-sa'la pulled him out of the river and he's cut up awful bad. He'll probably be all right if Su-ta'li can get some food down him."

"It's a good thing the big storm didn't push him farther down the big Hi-wass'ee," Talking Rock said. "By now he would be on his way to the ocean for certain."

"We need to get him back to the mission compound where we can take care of him properly," Talking Rock said.

"Maybe tomorrow," Corn Silk replied. "He's being treated very well here. My mother is quite good at this sort of thing. She doesn't want him moved for a while. One good sign is that he's been sweating."

Learning that Corn Silk had linkstered the trial, Taking Rock and Merlin were eager for details.

"Preacher Paul gave a marvelous testimony during his trial," Corn Silk said. "And despite his weakness and injuries, he was very articulate. His recital of the facts of Christianity and his obvious humility swayed all but one of the conjurers present. And A-sa'la says he himself wants to become a Christian."

"*He what?*" Merlin asked.

"That's the truth," Corn Silk said. "The Priest of Fire is impressed that Preacher Paul has a powerful God, one who performs miracles."

"Praise the Heavenly Father above!" Merlin said.

"But The Thunder is still angry and possibly some others who didn't get to attend."

Just as I started back into the cabin, an Indian runner came up and yelled out some some big news in Cherokee:

*"Caleb Clark has confessed setting the fire!"*

"The truth comes out!" Talking Rock yelled. "I suspected all along that Caleb was the culprit."

The runner reported that Conrad Carreker had placed Caleb under citizen's arrest at his blacksmith shop.

Talking Rock and Goliath Dan lit out to go there and Gu'li and I followed, along with Merlin. When we arrived, the farm worker was sitting in a side room with his head hanging low.

"Hey, Conrad, we just heard the news," Talking Rock said. "How did you get him to confess?"

"Didn't take much," Conrad Carreker said. "You'd done most of the detective work already. But during the past week Caleb kept coming around every day, wanting to talk, and I took time to listen to him. He looked right miserable as if he were carrying a heavy burden on his shoulders. When he came in today, he looked even worse and I invited him to take a seat, as always.

"He didn't get too far along before he broke down and started crying," Conrad continued. "Then he told me that, since the burning, all of his friends at the mission had turned against him. Even his Cherokee friends abandoned him. And his wife is about to leave him and take their kids. The final blow came when Preacher Paul refused to have anything more to do with him."

"In other words," Talking Rock said, "Caleb was right ready to confess?"

"For certain. So I advised him that it would be best for him to come right out and tell the whole story and plead for mercy and should turn himself in instead of waiting for the sheriff to come with an arrest warrant."

"God works His miracles in unusual ways," Merlin spoke up. "Hallelujah!"

"Yes indeed, Merlin," Conrad Carrreker said. "As Talking Rock suspected from the start, the idea for setting the torch to the town house came to Caleb after he heard one of Preacher Paul's strong sermons against the priests. To Caleb's twisted way of thinking, he felt if he burned down the building it would slow down the priests and would bring appreciation to him from Preacher Paul. Unfortunately, it did neither. It backfired and became a black mark against the entire mission community."

"I hope you obtained a statement from him—a confession."

"Yes, indeed. I've got it all written down. Among other things, Caleb wrote out an apology to the Cherokee head man at Eu-har'lee and also expressed his regret to all of the Cherokees in the valley. He wanted to let them know that it was him and him alone who was responsible for the fire and that none of the missionaries had anything to do with it, particularly not Preacher Paul."

"That should calm the minds of our Cherokee friends," Merlin said, "once they learn that the fire resulted from the sick mind of only one lone farm worker."

As Gu'li and I were walking home, I came up with an idea. "Wa-gu'li, why don't we get together all our friends and scholars at the mission and rebuild the town house for the Indians of Eu-har'lee?"

"Hey, that's a wonderful idea, T'san," Gu'li replied, "a great idea."

"Our folks know all about house-raisings," I said, "and we can get our carpenter, Hawkeye Hawkins, to be our work leader."

When we got home, I told Kindness and Goliath Dan what we'd been thinking.

"That would be a splendid gesture, boys," Kindness said.

Goliath Dan also expressed his delight and support. "I'm sure Merlin and Talking Rock and the whole missionary crowd would be delighted to help out in a big way."

So, early the following week, on a day set by Hawkeye, we sent runners up and down the valley announcing the house-raising. We were tickled when a bunch of Cherokees led by Oak Tree turned up to help us out plus the entire mission bunch, including a number of young scholars. We started work right after sunup, cutting the logs with axes and crosscut saws.

"We don't need nails," Hawkeye said. "We just need to get our logs notched so they fit properly."

After we finished raising the walls, Oak Tree chinked and daubed the log crevices with mud. Later, with guidance by Indian elders, the students built up the thatched roof.

By sundown we were tickled to death that the Cherokees had a beautiful new town house! Then we joined together in a big cookout, inviting everyone in the vicinity, to come join in the celebration: red, black and white.

Goliath Dan and Oak Tree roasted bear meat during the day and served it at twilight along with baked sweet potatoes plus corn cakes cooked in hickory nut oil and with sassafras tea to drink.

Everyone got their fill. Afterward, Talking Rock brought in his steer wagon and anchored it as a stage for a program. Head man Ta-wa'di the Hawk led off. "It's wonderful what has happened, and all so quickly," he said. "Thank you one and all."

He introduced the Priest of Fire for a few words, with Corn Silk doing the linkstering. "My friends, new and old," A-sa'la said, "this is truly heart rending, what has happened here today. Yesterday I started reading some passages in the New Testament published in Sequoyan Talking Leaves, and I am convinced that you missionaries are truly messengers from a God of Love. Thank you all for your love gift today to the people of Eu-har'lee and to all our people here in the valley." He received a big applause.

Merlin urged Preacher Paul to speak also. With a little help from Chief Ta-wa'di, the frail old missionary managed to struggle up from his seat.

"My dear friends, I'm mighty proud that from the terrible tragedy has come a wonderful reconciliation along with this beautiful new town house. I want to thank the original suggestion given to us by our young friends, Wa-gu'li and

T'san-us'di. And I wish to thank everyone concerned, especially the work leader, Mister Hawkeye Hawkins, and for every one's dedicated labor in rebuilding this town house."

"A-sa'la, sir," the old missionary continued, "we are humbled by your wonderful spirit." Then, amazingly, Preacher Paul reached over and gave the Priest of Fire a big hug right there in front of the whole crowd.

Merlin joined in the hugging, which lasted a good while. They were all shedding tears. It was a sight to see. I'm sorry Ma and Pa weren't alive to witness it, but I was happy knowing they saw it from heaven.

Then the Priest of Fire said, "Preacher Paul, if you will permit me, I wish to become a candidate to join your church. Several of my followers may wish to do the same."

"Hallelujah and praise the Lord! " the old missionary said. "We'll be most honored to have you and all your friends."

To wind it up, Merlin got up and ended the celebration by leading us all in singing a favorite hymn:

*There's a wideness in God's mercy*
*Like the wideness of the sea.*
*There's a kindness in His justice,*
*Which is more than liberty.*

*For the love of God is broader*
*Than the measure of man's mind;*
*And the heart of the Eternal*
*Is most wonderfully kind.*

Well sir, there weren't many dry eyes in the crowd that night, watching Preacher Paul and A-sa'la showing such affection for one another and witnessing the appreciative faces of the Cherokees.

As we walked home that night by the light of the moon, Wa-gu'li and I couldn't stop talking about what a miracle God had given us—the miracle of Christian love—enabling us to right a wrong in our neighborhood. My buddy Gu'li even said he might want to get Merlin to baptize him sometime in the future.

"Wonderful," I said.

"I'm giving it serious thought," Guli said.

# CHAPTER THIRTY

## Su-Tal'li Baptized, gets a New Name

Gu'li ran up to our cabin, full of excitement. "T'san, Su-ta'li is joining the Jesus God church!" he said as he walked in.

I couldn't get over Wa-gu'li calling his ma by her given name, but I knew it was common among Cherokees when speaking about their parents.

"I could tell it was coming," Gu'li said. "I'd been with her on several occasions when she would sob while looking at the painting of Jesus there on the wall in the church, the one of him hanging on the cross, bleeding and suffering before he died."

"Su-ta'li, what does it all mean?" Gu'li had asked his

mother. "His death on the cross, I mean."

"My child, don't you see? Christ's sacrificial death canceled all of my sins of the past. Everyone's sins. They are forgiven. I am free. I have become a new person, one of God's children."

"What god?"

"The Father, the Son, and the Holy Spirit. It's called the Trinity. Some day you will understand, son, and will believe just as I do and your brother Corn Silk does."

From then on, Gu'li and I noticed that she seemed to in a state of supreme joy. Several times a day she would put her hands together, like a church steeple, lift her gaze to the sky and say, "Praise be to God, for all of His mercies."

Merlin noticed it also. He told me that Su-ta'li, a woman of quiet dignity, "has been carrying herself lately with increasing serenity and stateliness."

I got the feeling that even the chastened Preacher Paul—now recovering from the wounds incurred in his awful ride down the river—must have had a tug in his heart for the tall Su-ta'li, being thankful that she was cleaning her mind of earlier beliefs in the animal and river spirits, as taught by the full-blood priests.

I myself had become a great admirer of Su-ta'li, not just because she was the mother of my friend Gu'li, but because of her tough determination on every task she undertook. And besides that, she was a great cook.

I reckoned that Su-ta'li had been a real beauty in her younger days. She had borne four children, a large family for the Cherokees, who averaged only two or three offspring, but one had died in childbirth and another of consumption, leaving only Corn Silk, her eldest, and Wa-gu'li, the youngest. And then in 1814, as I mentioned, she lost her husband, *Ahuh-hee'lee*, Jim Eagle, who was killed fighting with Colonel Morgan's Cherokee Regiment in the battle at Horseshoe Bend.

While her bronze face was a bit wrinkled, Su-ta'li's long black hair remained smooth and silky. And her hands carried a beauty of their own, particularly when she gently touched the painting of Jesus on the cross. It also showed when she reached out to pat Wa-gu'li on his back, pausing to run her loving fingers through his black hair.

When she started attending the mission classes, I sensed a youthful renewal that was noticed also by her kin and neighbors living in the upper end of the valley.

"Su-ta'li is learning to become a child of God," they said. "She is taking more time to read her Cherokee New Testament and she has become more gentle and forgiving to her friends as well as her two boys."

"She prays devoutly each day for everyone she can think of," Wa-gu'li said, "even those she considers her enemies, including the conjurer priests who in former months had become threatening when they heard of her new turn toward the Jesus God religion."

Corn Silk put it another way. "Su-ta'li appears to be putting behind her the memories of her difficult childhood and the trials and tribulations while rearing four children, and is taking on a new life as a Christian."

Merlin arranged for Su-ta'li to join the next training

class that would lead to baptizing. She was among five potential converts in training, including A-Sa'la, the former Priest of Fire. After completing the course, she received a little quiz from Merlin:

"Su-ta'li, do you think you've been saved by the grace of God?"

"Yes, Missionary."

"What have you done this week to merit being a member of Christ's Kingdom?"

"I prayed for all my neighbors, for their souls, and I read several chapters in the book of Matthew, using our talking leaves New Testament."

"Very good, Su-ta'li," he said. "You will be scheduled for the next baptism."

"One of her great attributes during the schooling," Merlin said, "was that, years before, she had learned English from her husband Jim Eagle, a mixed-breed who had died at Horseshoe Bend."

I asked Merlin about A-Sa'la.

"He's coming along very well," he said, "and it looks like we will be baptizing him in the next group of candidates."

Then came the great day of Su-ta'li's baptism.

I spent the night before with Wa-gu'li. On Baptism day Su-ta'li woke us up early, having arisen herself much earlier to prepare for the big occasion.

On the way to the church, Wa-gu'li and Corn Silk took

great pains protecting their mother's white dress, keeping it from touching the water as she forded shallow streams going to the baptismal spot on Persimmon Creek. Three neighborhood youngsters ran ahead of her to hold back the long limbs, bushes and brambles sticking out along the way.

Following us was another candidate for baptism, Little Arrowhead, age ten, from the same area. She, too, was dressed in a white frock. She was accompanied by her mother and two siblings.

Our happy little crowd laughed and talked as we walked, covering the distance in less than a half hour, encountering only a few deer and wild turkeys along the way. As we arrived, all the candidates were greeted by Preacher Paul, Missionary Merlin, and Reverend Bushyred, who was visiting from Tenn-a'see.

Meanwhile, Cherokees also were arriving from all directions. Among the fifty-odd people there was A-sa'la Car-te'kee and two other former priests, and a sprinkling of blacks, including a black woman with ebony black skin and pearly-white teeth. She was Eula, Trader Murphy's housekeeper.

"Su-ta'li, you look wonderful," Missionary Merlin told her as she arrived.

"You *all* look wonderful in your white dresses," added Preacher Paul, being linkstered by Cherokee exhorter Bushyred.

Corn Silk, Gu'li and I found seats on the river bank. The three ministers, all dressed in white, led the white-frocked

candidates single file down the trail to the creek, followed
by the throng. On the way down, everyone sang, "Come
Holy Spirit, Dove Divine."

I recognized the site as one of our old swimming holes.
The crystal clear waters were about about four and a half
feet deep and underneath a sheet of solid rock on the bottom.

While the singing continued, the ministers eased their
way into the water, followed by the candidates, with the quiet waters swirling softly up over their waist bands.

The choir ended their singing. And with Reverend Bushyred doing the linkerstering, Preacher Paul had opening re-
marks.

"My friends," he said, "this is a sacred ceremony symbol-
izing a new beginning for each of the candidates. They are
being washed with the blood of the Lamb and will come
out spotless in soul and body, as white as their gowns."

The singers on the river bank began a new song. It was a
mournful chant, but I could see that Su-ta'li was enjoying
it, even though she had her eyes closed.

Missionary Merlin called for the candidates to step forward for baptism. Su-ta'li was first in line.

I felt for her. She told us later that her heart was pounding. Just then, as she raised her head and gazed up on the
bank and saw the three of us looking on, her courage appeared to strengthen. She edged toward Missionary Mer-

lin, placing both of her hands on the minister's left fore-arm. Su-ta'li closed her eyes and heard the missionary say as he raised his right hand:

"*My beloved Sister, Su-ta'li, I baptize you in the name of the Father, the Son and the Holy Ghost. Baptized in sin, raised to eternal life.*"

Just as her head went under the water, she told us later, "I felt I was floating in time." She quickly rose to the surface, opened her eyes, blinking in the sunlight and then winked at those of us on the bank!

Merlin announced, "Su-ta'li, now you have a new name. In the future we will call you Mary, Christian Mary. You are being named for one of the great women of the Bible, Mary Magdalene, who loved Jesus so very much and who lovingly washed his feet in oil. You will henceforth be called *Christian Mary*."

As she walked out of the water, Corn Silk and Wa-gu'li wrapped her in a warm bearskin.

"*Christian Mary*," she kept repeating the words, ". . . *Christian Mary…*"

I could see that she could hardly wait until she got back home to tell her villagers about her new name: "*Mary. . . Christian Mary!*" On the way she repeated the name several times.

Gu'li and I ran closely behind to join in the big celebration to follow. It would be a night to remember.

Joseph E. ("Joe") Dabney (1929–2015) has received national attention for his books, *Mountain Spirits, More Mountain Spirits, HERK, The Food, Folklore and Art of Lowcountry Cooking* and *Smokehouse Ham, Spoon Bread & Scuppernong Wine.*

*Smokehouse* won the prestigious James Beard Foundation's top book prize in 1999, "Cookbook of the Year," considered the "Oscar" of food world literature. Beard Awards Chairman Nach Waxman called it, "The best of the best, a book that makes an important, lasting contribution to food literature and culture."

After 20 printings, an expanded 500-page Tenth Anniversary Edition of *Smokehouse* was published in 2008 by Cumberland House, an imprint of Sourcebooks. A trade paperback edition of the anniversary book was released in 2010.

Also in 2010, Cumberland House/Sourcebooks released Dabney's latest, another "cultural cookbook"—*The Food, Folklore & Art of Lowcountry Cooking*—to outstanding reviews." The book was subsequently nominated by the James Beard Foundation in its 2011 American Food category.

*TIME* Magazine described Dabney's first book, *Mountain Spirits* (Scribner) as "a splendid and sometimes hilarious history" of the Southeastern hill country culture. He appeared on the NBC *Today Show*, being interviewed by Gene Shalit, and was subsequently elected a "Knight of Mark Twain" by the *Mark Twain Journal.*

On the basis of his folklore books, he was awarded the 2005 Jack Daniel's Lifetime Achievement Award by the Southern Foodways Alliance at the University of Mississippi in Oxford. Earlier, the Friends of the Dunwoody Library in north Atlanta also honored him with its Brooke Baker Award for Lifetime Achievement.

Dabney was a native of South Carolina, a graduate of Berry College and a veteran of the Korean War. His early career was in journalism. He served on several newspapers in the South including the *Florence* (SC) *Morning News* (associate editor), the Gainesville, GA, *Daily Times* (managing editor) and *The Atlanta Journal* (state editor).

Dabney joined the Lockheed-Georgia Company in 1965 as editor of its employee newspaper. He later became a public relations representative, handling the aerospace firm's worldwide PR on the C-130 and C-5 transport aircraft, from which job he is retired after a 24-year career there. He is also the author of *HERK*, the 500-page definitive biography of the Lockheed C-130 transport aircraft.

Dabney and his wife Susanne resided in the new City of Brookhaven in north Atlanta and were the parents of five grown children. They were members of Dunwoody Baptist Church. Dabney was former president of the church's Young at Heart seniors organization and sang in the church's Heartstrings senior choir. *Cherokee Valley So Wild* was his first book of fiction.

CPSIA information can be obtained at www.ICGtesting.com
Printed in the USA
LVOW11s0137200816

500759LV00004B/5/P